0 1197 0731357 1

INDESTRUCTIBLE
HULK

AGENT OF S.H.I.E.L.D.

VOLUME 01

INDESTRUCTIBLE HULK VOL. 1: AGENT OF S.H.I.E.L.D. Contains material originally published in magazine form as INDESTRUCTIBLE HULK #1-5. First printing 2013. ISBN# 978-0-7851-6831-7. Published by MARVEL WORLDWIDE, INC., a subsidiary of MARVEL ENTERTAINMENT, LLC. OFFICE OF PUBLICATION: 135 West 50th Street, New York, NY 10020. Copyright © 2012 and 2013 Marvel Characters, Inc. All rights reserved. All characters featured in this issue and the distinctive names and likenesses thereof, and all related indicia are trademarks of Marvel Characters, Inc. No similarity between any of the names, characters, persons, and/or institutions in this magazine with those of any living or dead person or institution is intended, and any such similarity which may exist is purely coincidental. **Printed in the U.S.A.** ALAN FINE, EVP - Office of the President, Marvel Worldwide, Inc. and EVP & CMO Marvel Characters B.V.; DAN BUCKLEY, Publisher & President - Print, Animation & Digital Divisions; JOE QUESADA, Chief Creative Officer; TOM BREVOORT, SVP of Publishing; DAVID BOGART, SVP of Operations & Procurement, Publishing; C.B. CEBULSKI, SVP of Creator & Content Development; DAVID GABRIEL, SVP of Print & Digital Publishing Sales; JIM O'KEEFE, VP of Operations & Logistics; DAN CARR, Executive Director of Publishing Technology; SUSAN CRESPI, Editorial Operations Manager; ALEX MORALES, Publishing Operations Manager; STAN LEE, Chairman Emeritus. For information regarding advertising in Marvel Comics or on Marvel.com, please contact Niza Disla, Director of Marvel Partnerships, at ndisla@marvel.com. For Marvel subscription inquiries, please call 800-217-9158. **Manufactured between 3/18/2013 and 4/29/2013 by R.R. DONNELLEY, INC., SALEM, VA, USA.**

10 9 8 7 6 5 4 3 2 1

WRITER
MARK WAID
PENCILER
LEINIL FRANCIS YU
INKER
GERRY ALANGUILAN
COLORIST
SUNNY GHO
LETTERER
CHRIS ELIOPOULOS
COVER ARTIST
LEINIL FRANCIS YU
WITH **SUNNY GHO** & **VAL STAPLES**
ASSISTANT EDITOR
JON MOISAN
EDITOR
MARK PANICCIA

COLLECTION EDITOR
CORY LEVINE
ASSISTANT EDITORS
ALEX STARBUCK
NELSON RIBEIRO
EDITORS, SPECIAL PROJECTS
JENNIFER GRÜNWALD
MARK D. BEAZLEY

SENIOR EDITOR,
SPECIAL PROJECTS
JEFF YOUNGQUIST
SVP OF PRINT & DIGITAL
PUBLISHING SALES
DAVID GABRIEL
BOOK DESIGN
JEFF POWELL & **CORY LEVINE**

EDITOR IN CHIEF
AXEL ALONSO
CHIEF CREATIVE OFFICER
JOE QUESADA
PUBLISHER
DAN BUCKLEY
EXECUTIVE PRODUCER
ALAN FINE

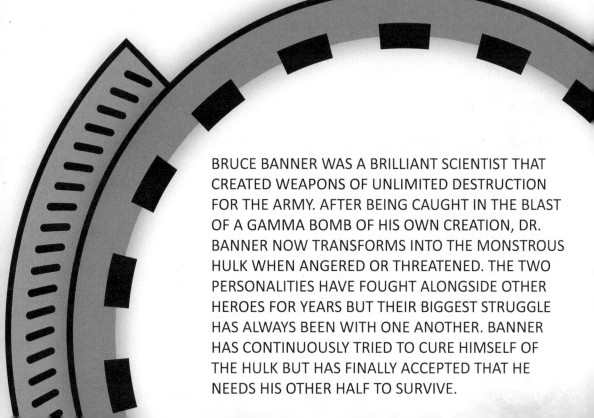

BRUCE BANNER WAS A BRILLIANT SCIENTIST THAT CREATED WEAPONS OF UNLIMITED DESTRUCTION FOR THE ARMY. AFTER BEING CAUGHT IN THE BLAST OF A GAMMA BOMB OF HIS OWN CREATION, DR. BANNER NOW TRANSFORMS INTO THE MONSTROUS HULK WHEN ANGERED OR THREATENED. THE TWO PERSONALITIES HAVE FOUGHT ALONGSIDE OTHER HEROES FOR YEARS BUT THEIR BIGGEST STRUGGLE HAS ALWAYS BEEN WITH ONE ANOTHER. BANNER HAS CONTINUOUSLY TRIED TO CURE HIMSELF OF THE HULK BUT HAS FINALLY ACCEPTED THAT HE NEEDS HIS OTHER HALF TO SURVIVE.

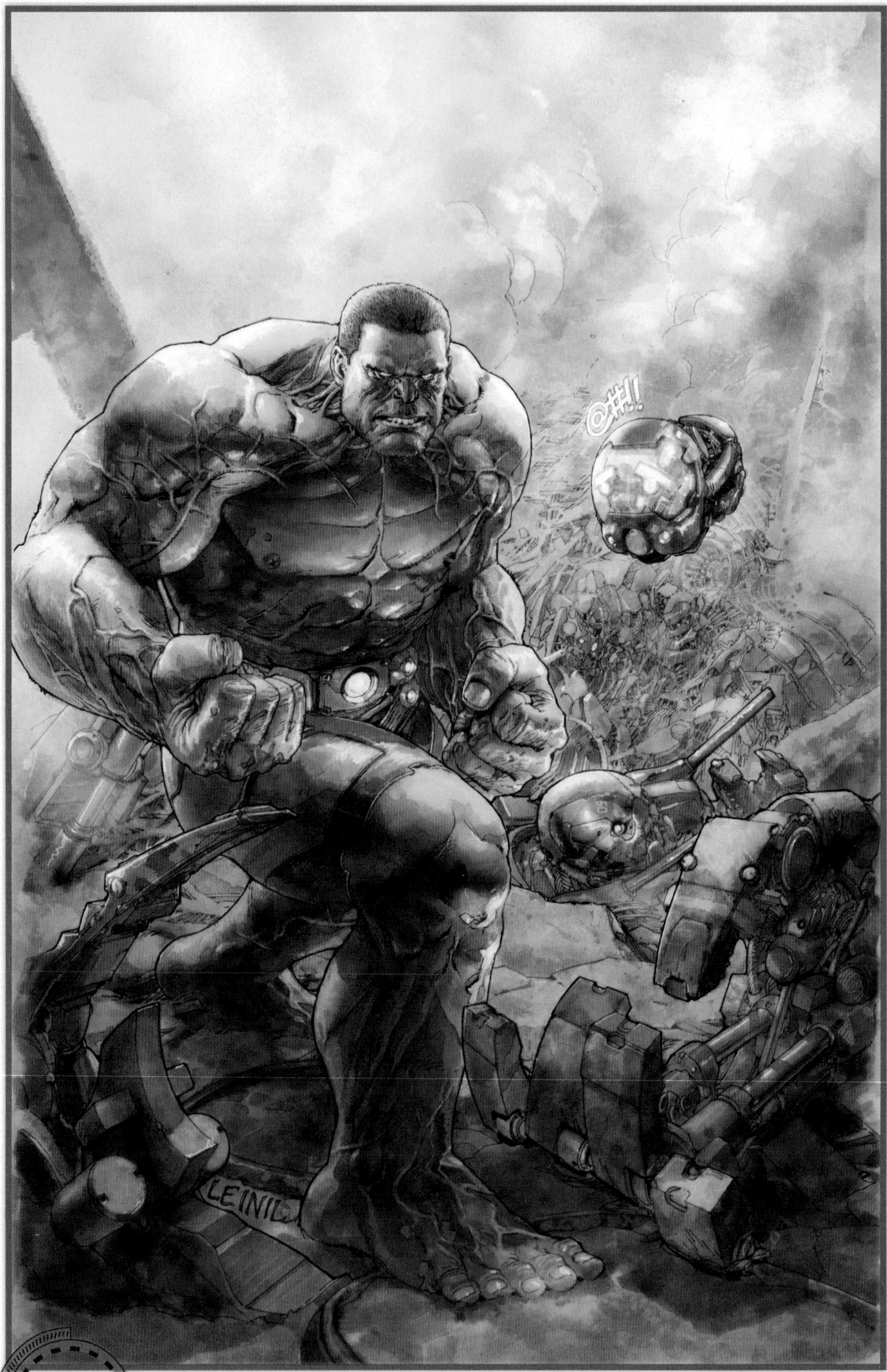

@#!!
LEINIL

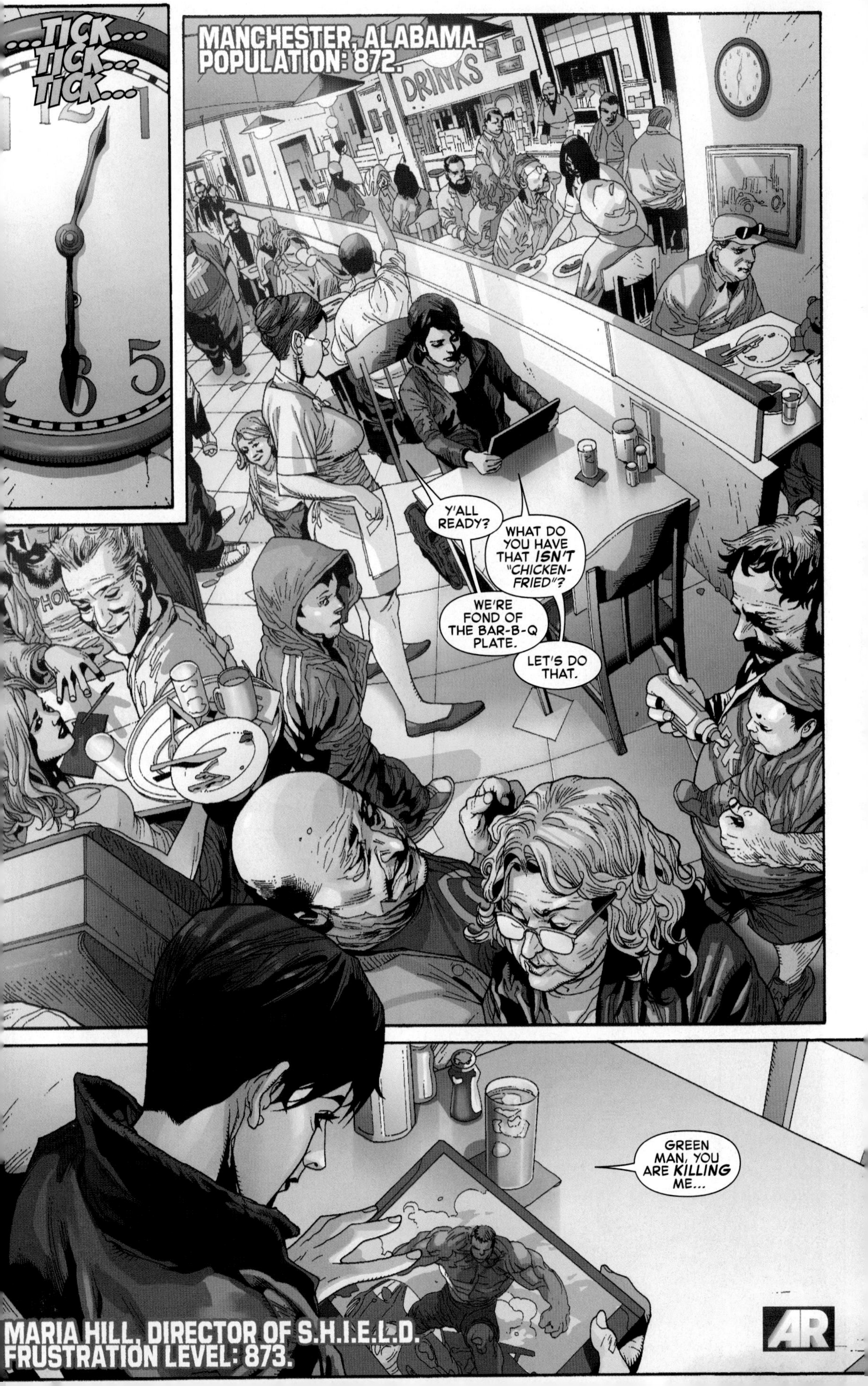
...TICK...
TICK...
TICK...
MANCHESTER, ALABAMA.
POPULATION: 872.
DRINKS
Y'ALL READY?
WHAT DO YOU HAVE THAT ISN'T "CHICKEN-FRIED"?
WE'RE FOND OF THE BAR-B-Q PLATE.
LET'S DO THAT.
GREEN MAN, YOU ARE KILLING ME...
MARIA HILL, DIRECTOR OF S.H.I.E.L.D.
FRUSTRATION LEVEL: 873.

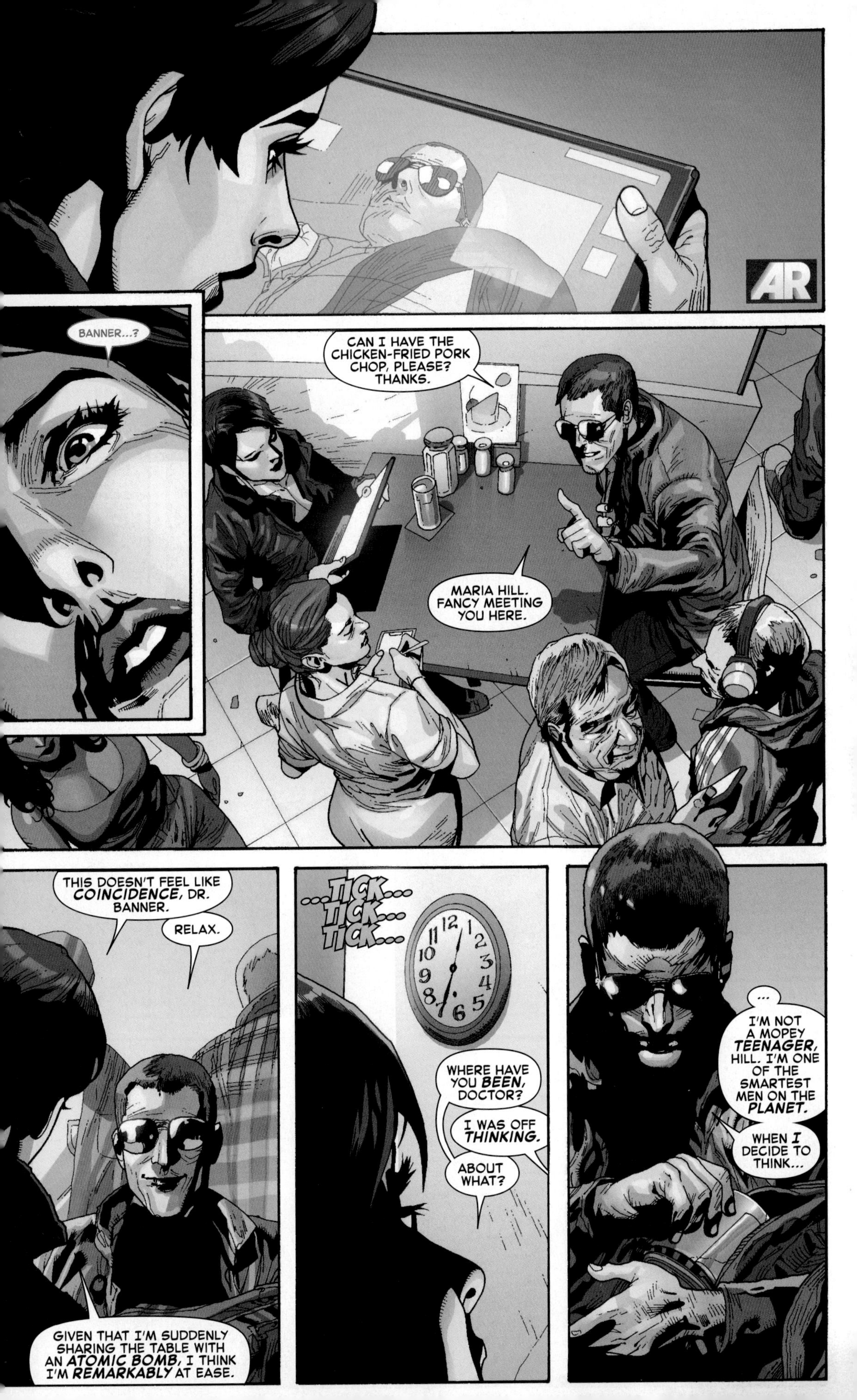
AR
BANNER...?
CAN I HAVE THE CHICKEN-FRIED PORK CHOP, PLEASE? THANKS.
MARIA HILL. FANCY MEETING YOU HERE.
THIS DOESN'T FEEL LIKE COINCIDENCE, DR. BANNER.
RELAX.
GIVEN THAT I'M SUDDENLY SHARING THE TABLE WITH AN ATOMIC BOMB, I THINK I'M REMARKABLY AT EASE.
...TICK... TICK... TICK...
WHERE HAVE YOU BEEN, DOCTOR?
I WAS OFF THINKING.
ABOUT WHAT?
...
I'M NOT A MOPEY TEENAGER, HILL. I'M ONE OF THE SMARTEST MEN ON THE PLANET.
WHEN I DECIDE TO THINK...

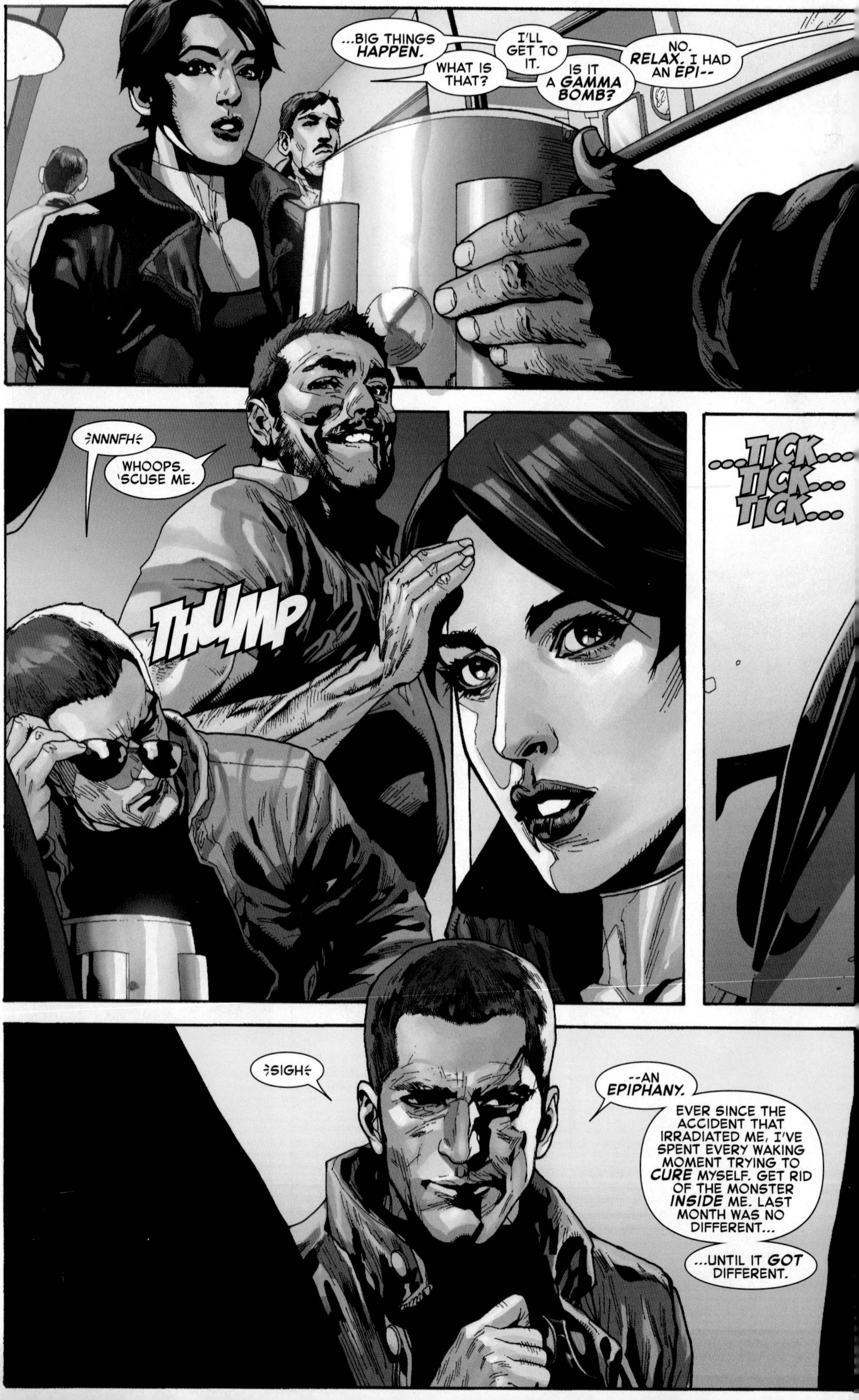
...BIG THINGS HAPPEN.
WHAT IS THAT?
I'LL GET TO IT.
IS IT A GAMMA BOMB?
NO. RELAX. I HAD AN EPI--
›NNNFH‹
WHOOPS. 'SCUSE ME.
THUMP
...TICK... TICK... TICK...
›SIGH‹
--AN EPIPHANY.
EVER SINCE THE ACCIDENT THAT IRRADIATED ME, I'VE SPENT EVERY WAKING MOMENT TRYING TO CURE MYSELF. GET RID OF THE MONSTER INSIDE ME. LAST MONTH WAS NO DIFFERENT...
...UNTIL IT GOT DIFFERENT.

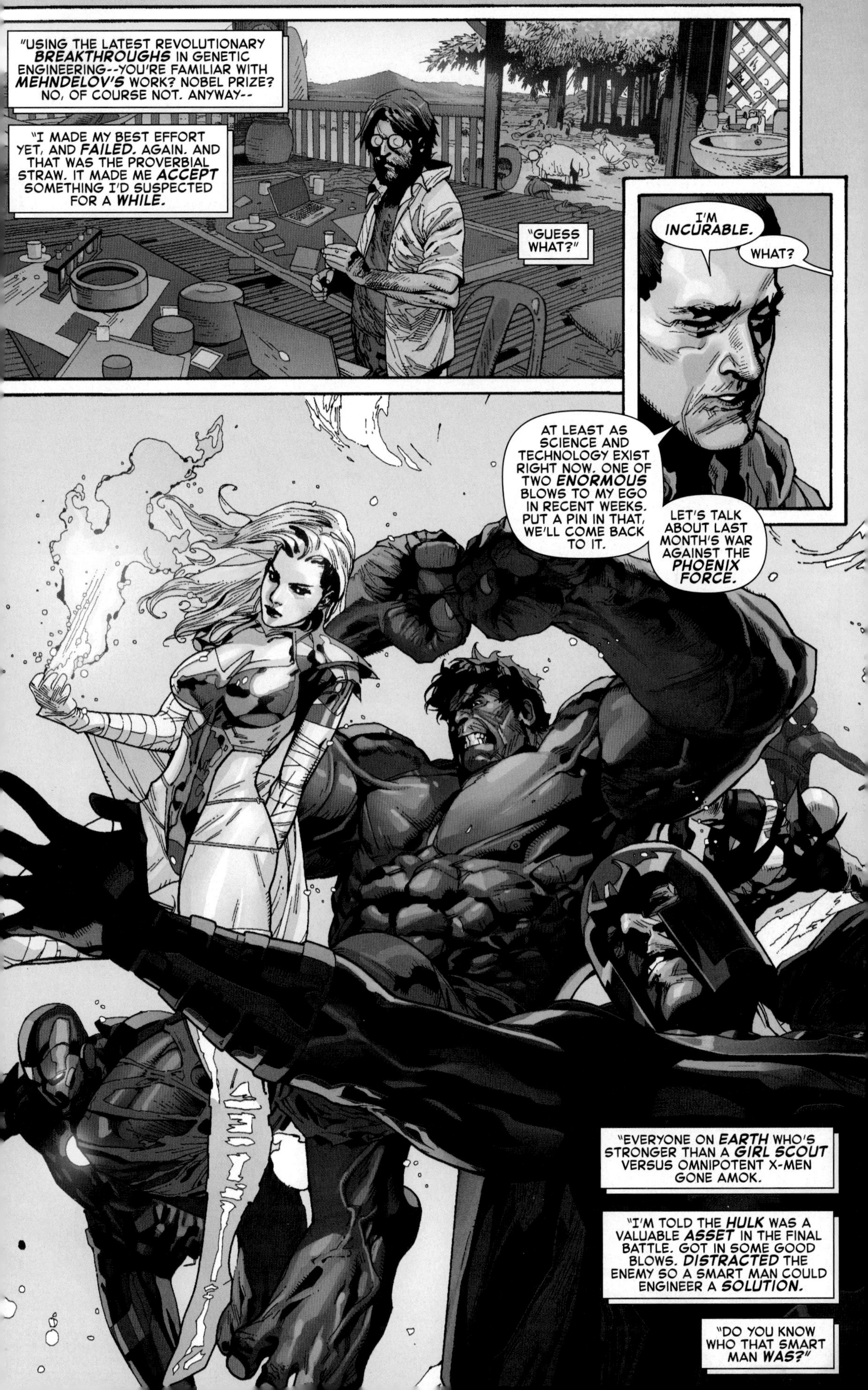
"USING THE LATEST REVOLUTIONARY BREAKTHROUGHS IN GENETIC ENGINEERING--YOU'RE FAMILIAR WITH MEHNDELOV'S WORK? NOBEL PRIZE? NO, OF COURSE NOT. ANYWAY--
"I MADE MY BEST EFFORT YET, AND FAILED. AGAIN. AND THAT WAS THE PROVERBIAL STRAW. IT MADE ME ACCEPT SOMETHING I'D SUSPECTED FOR A WHILE.
"GUESS WHAT?"
I'M INCURABLE.
WHAT?
AT LEAST AS SCIENCE AND TECHNOLOGY EXIST RIGHT NOW. ONE OF TWO ENORMOUS BLOWS TO MY EGO IN RECENT WEEKS. PUT A PIN IN THAT, WE'LL COME BACK TO IT.
LET'S TALK ABOUT LAST MONTH'S WAR AGAINST THE PHOENIX FORCE.
"EVERYONE ON EARTH WHO'S STRONGER THAN A GIRL SCOUT VERSUS OMNIPOTENT X-MEN GONE AMOK.
"I'M TOLD THE HULK WAS A VALUABLE ASSET IN THE FINAL BATTLE. GOT IN SOME GOOD BLOWS. DISTRACTED THE ENEMY SO A SMART MAN COULD ENGINEER A SOLUTION.
"DO YOU KNOW WHO THAT SMART MAN WAS?"

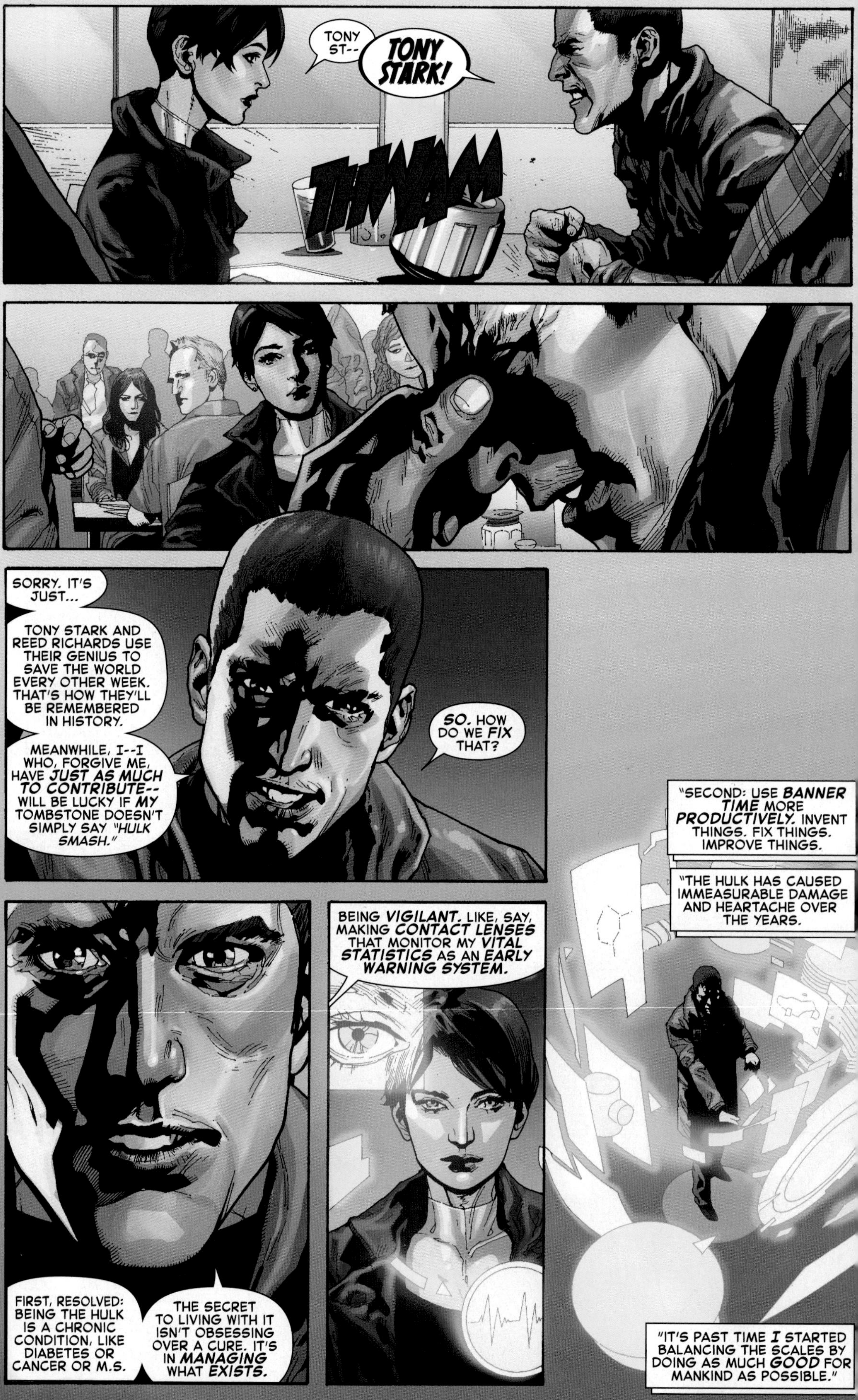
TONY ST--
TONY STARK!
THWAM
SORRY. IT'S JUST...
TONY STARK AND REED RICHARDS USE THEIR GENIUS TO SAVE THE WORLD EVERY OTHER WEEK. THAT'S HOW THEY'LL BE REMEMBERED IN HISTORY.
MEANWHILE, I--I WHO, FORGIVE ME, HAVE JUST AS MUCH TO CONTRIBUTE-- WILL BE LUCKY IF MY TOMBSTONE DOESN'T SIMPLY SAY "HULK SMASH."
SO. HOW DO WE FIX THAT?
FIRST, RESOLVED: BEING THE HULK IS A CHRONIC CONDITION, LIKE DIABETES OR CANCER OR M.S.
THE SECRET TO LIVING WITH IT ISN'T OBSESSING OVER A CURE. IT'S IN MANAGING WHAT EXISTS.
BEING VIGILANT. LIKE, SAY, MAKING CONTACT LENSES THAT MONITOR MY VITAL STATISTICS AS AN EARLY WARNING SYSTEM.
"SECOND: USE BANNER TIME MORE PRODUCTIVELY. INVENT THINGS. FIX THINGS. IMPROVE THINGS.
"THE HULK HAS CAUSED IMMEASURABLE DAMAGE AND HEARTACHE OVER THE YEARS.
"IT'S PAST TIME I STARTED BALANCING THE SCALES BY DOING AS MUCH GOOD FOR MANKIND AS POSSIBLE."

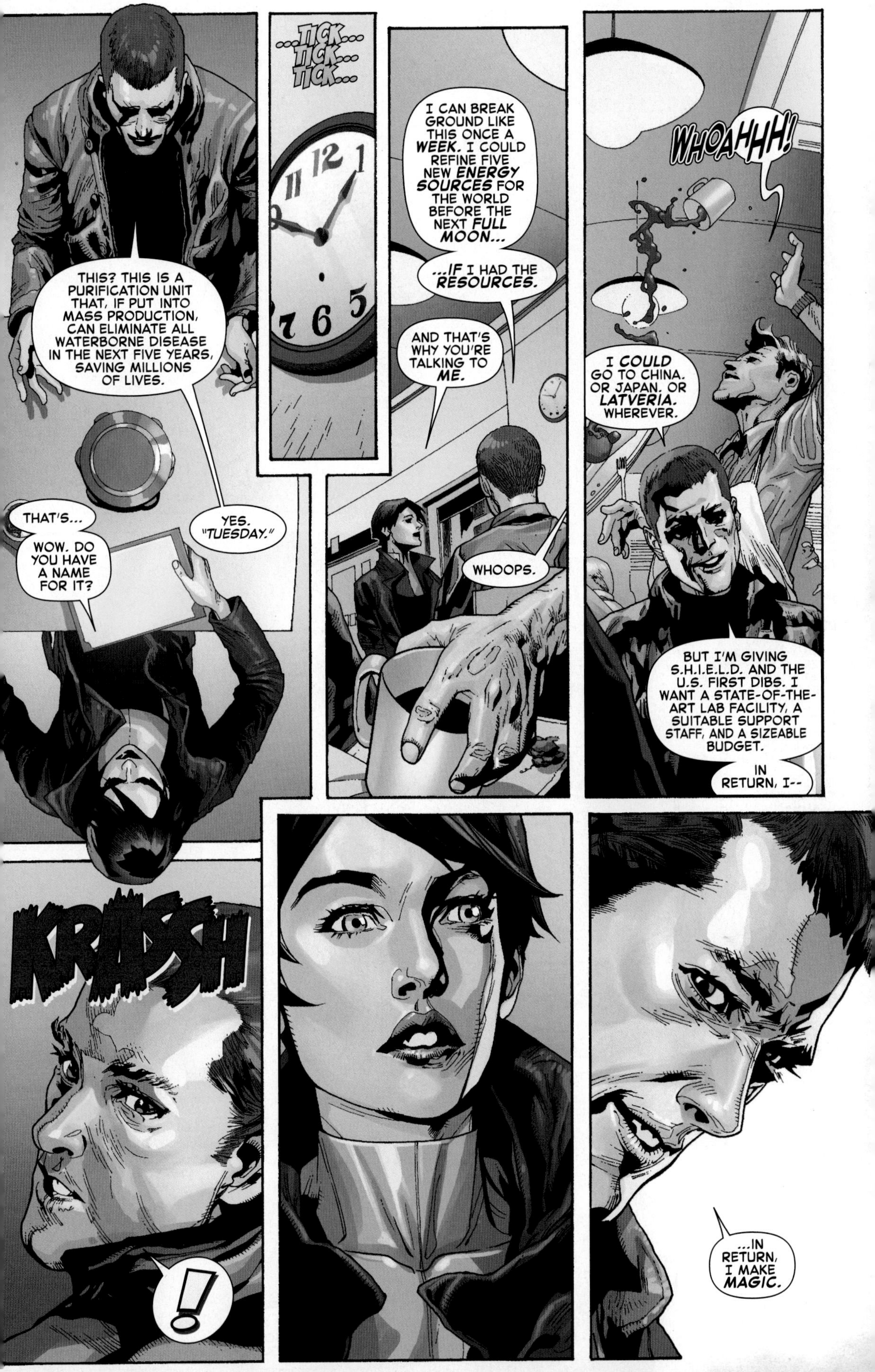
THIS? THIS IS A PURIFICATION UNIT THAT, IF PUT INTO MASS PRODUCTION, CAN ELIMINATE ALL WATERBORNE DISEASE IN THE NEXT FIVE YEARS, SAVING MILLIONS OF LIVES.
THAT'S...
WOW. DO YOU HAVE A NAME FOR IT?
YES. "TUESDAY."
...TICK... TICK... TICK...
I CAN BREAK GROUND LIKE THIS ONCE A WEEK. I COULD REFINE FIVE NEW ENERGY SOURCES FOR THE WORLD BEFORE THE NEXT FULL MOON...
...IF I HAD THE RESOURCES.
AND THAT'S WHY YOU'RE TALKING TO ME.
WHOOPS.
WHOAHHH!
I COULD GO TO CHINA. OR JAPAN. OR LATVERIA. WHEREVER.
BUT I'M GIVING S.H.I.E.L.D. AND THE U.S. FIRST DIBS. I WANT A STATE-OF-THE-ART LAB FACILITY, A SUITABLE SUPPORT STAFF, AND A SIZEABLE BUDGET.
IN RETURN, I--
KRASH
!
...IN RETURN, I MAKE MAGIC.

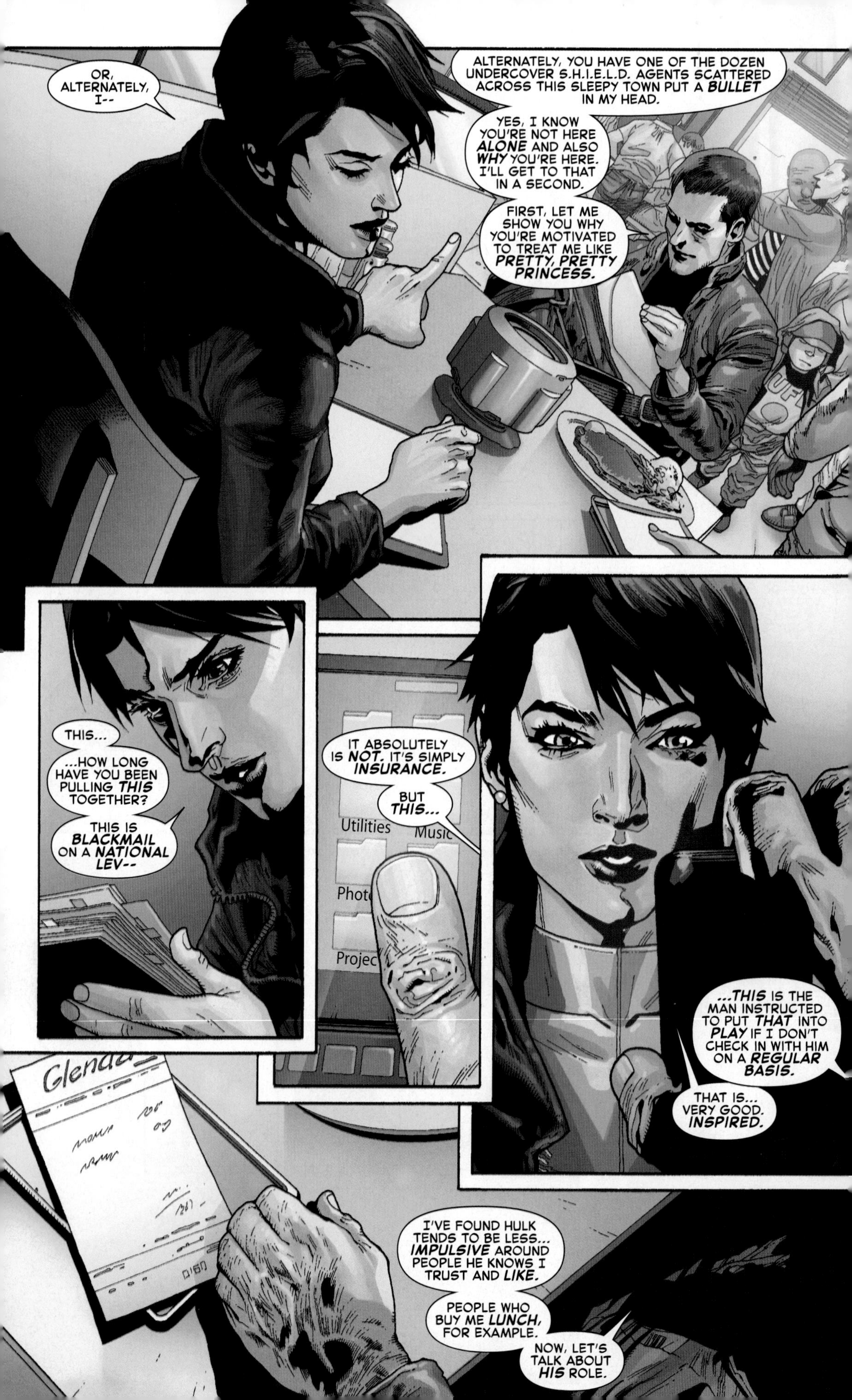
OR, ALTERNATELY, I--
ALTERNATELY, YOU HAVE ONE OF THE DOZEN UNDERCOVER S.H.I.E.L.D. AGENTS SCATTERED ACROSS THIS SLEEPY TOWN PUT A BULLET IN MY HEAD.
YES, I KNOW YOU'RE NOT HERE ALONE AND ALSO WHY YOU'RE HERE. I'LL GET TO THAT IN A SECOND.
FIRST, LET ME SHOW YOU WHY YOU'RE MOTIVATED TO TREAT ME LIKE PRETTY, PRETTY PRINCESS.
THIS...
...HOW LONG HAVE YOU BEEN PULLING THIS TOGETHER?
THIS IS BLACKMAIL ON A NATIONAL LEV--
IT ABSOLUTELY IS NOT. IT'S SIMPLY INSURANCE.
BUT THIS...
Utilities
Music
...THIS IS THE MAN INSTRUCTED TO PUT THAT INTO PLAY IF I DON'T CHECK IN WITH HIM ON A REGULAR BASIS.
THAT IS... VERY GOOD. INSPIRED.
Glenda
I'VE FOUND HULK TENDS TO BE LESS... IMPULSIVE AROUND PEOPLE HE KNOWS I TRUST AND LIKE.
PEOPLE WHO BUY ME LUNCH, FOR EXAMPLE.
NOW, LET'S TALK ABOUT HIS ROLE.

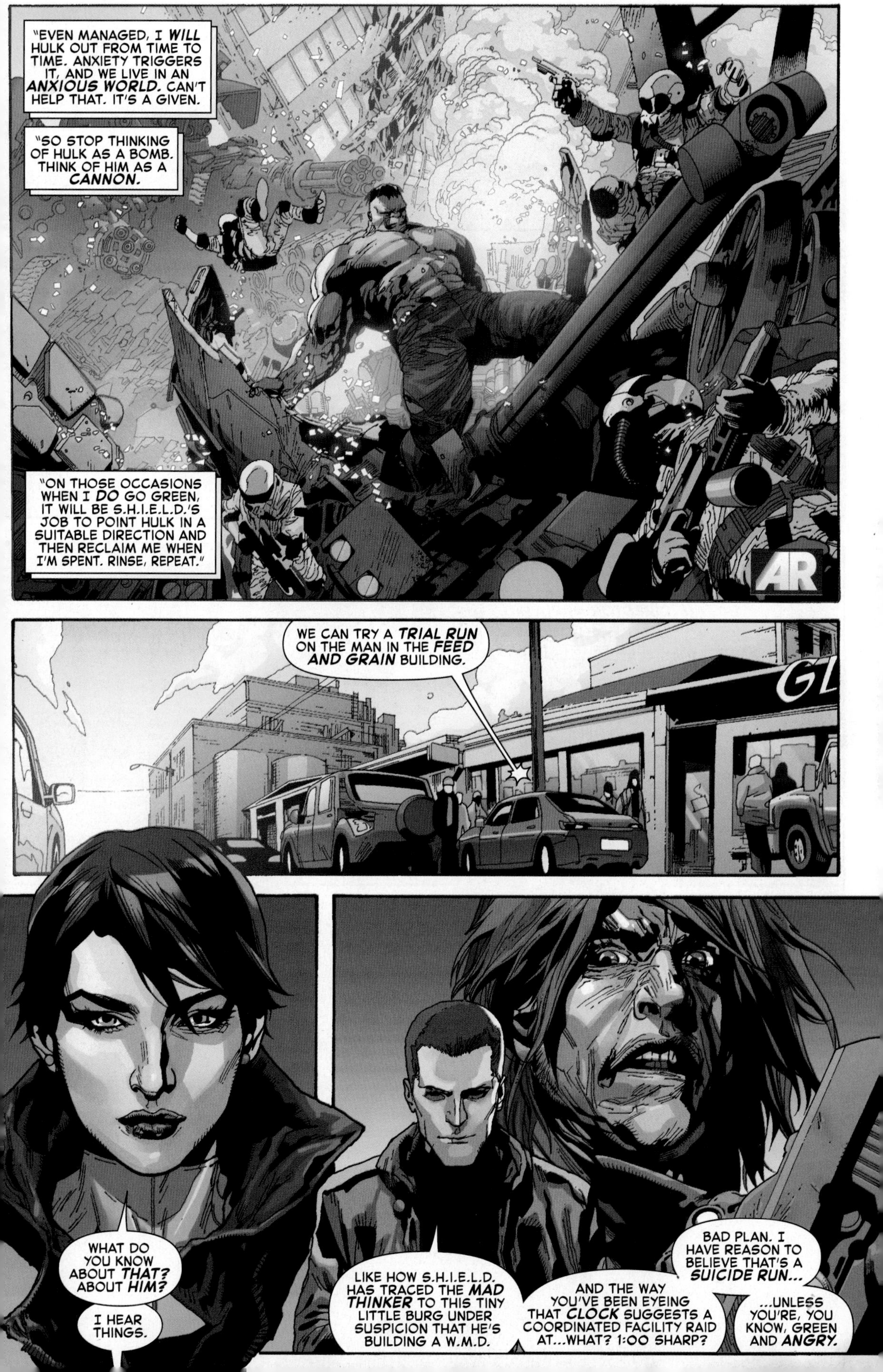
"EVEN MANAGED, I WILL HULK OUT FROM TIME TO TIME. ANXIETY TRIGGERS IT, AND WE LIVE IN AN ANXIOUS WORLD. CAN'T HELP THAT. IT'S A GIVEN.
"SO STOP THINKING OF HULK AS A BOMB. THINK OF HIM AS A CANNON.
"ON THOSE OCCASIONS WHEN I DO GO GREEN, IT WILL BE S.H.I.E.L.D.'S JOB TO POINT HULK IN A SUITABLE DIRECTION AND THEN RECLAIM ME WHEN I'M SPENT. RINSE, REPEAT."
AR
WE CAN TRY A TRIAL RUN ON THE MAN IN THE FEED AND GRAIN BUILDING.
WHAT DO YOU KNOW ABOUT THAT? ABOUT HIM?
I HEAR THINGS.
LIKE HOW S.H.I.E.L.D. HAS TRACED THE MAD THINKER TO THIS TINY LITTLE BURG UNDER SUSPICION THAT HE'S BUILDING A W.M.D.
AND THE WAY YOU'VE BEEN EYEING THAT CLOCK SUGGESTS A COORDINATED FACILITY RAID AT...WHAT? 1:00 SHARP?
BAD PLAN. I HAVE REASON TO BELIEVE THAT'S A SUICIDE RUN...
...UNLESS YOU'RE, YOU KNOW, GREEN AND ANGRY.

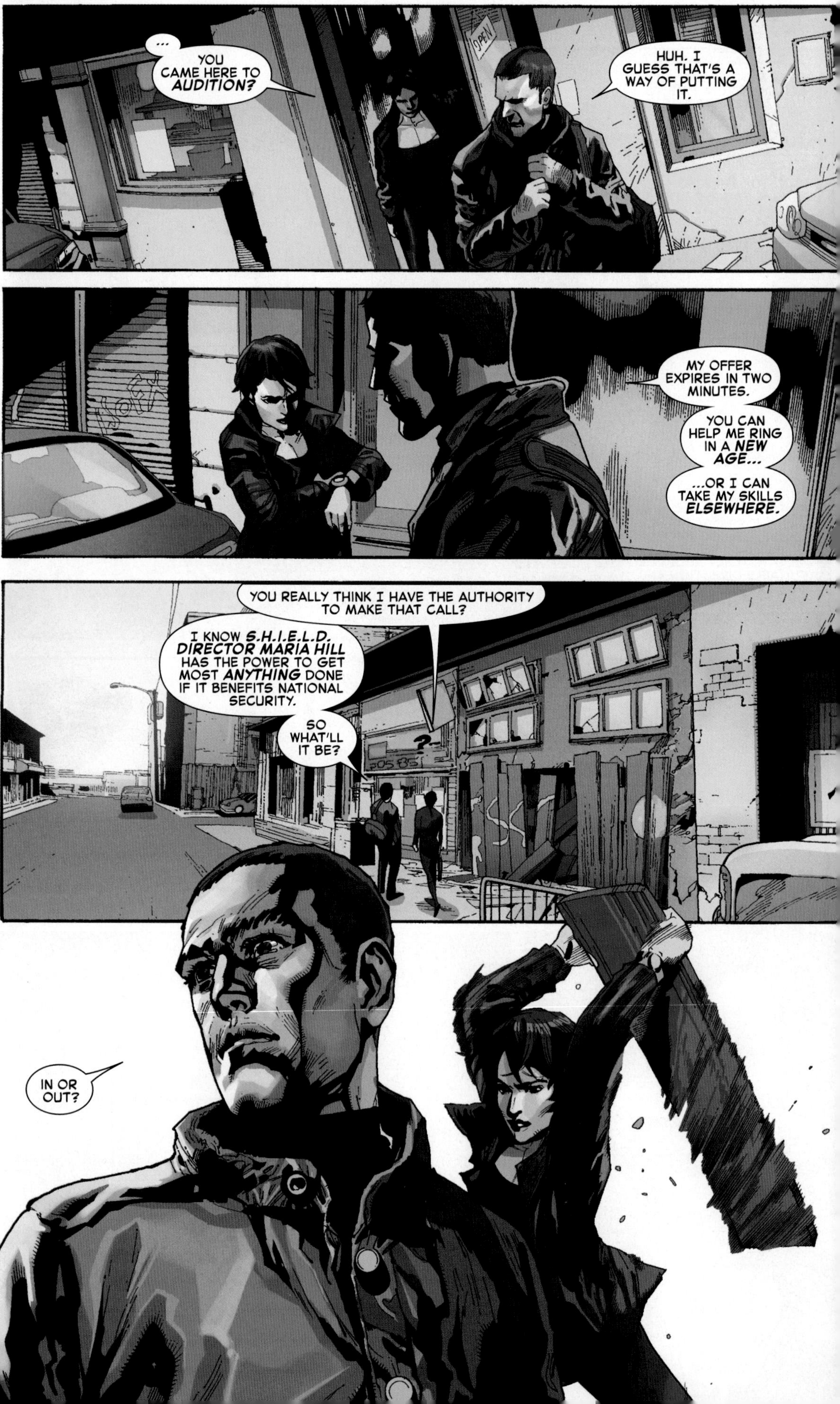
...
YOU CAME HERE TO AUDITION?
HUH. I GUESS THAT'S A WAY OF PUTTING IT.
MY OFFER EXPIRES IN TWO MINUTES.
YOU CAN HELP ME RING IN A NEW AGE...
...OR I CAN TAKE MY SKILLS ELSEWHERE.
YOU REALLY THINK I HAVE THE AUTHORITY TO MAKE THAT CALL?
I KNOW S.H.I.E.L.D. DIRECTOR MARIA HILL HAS THE POWER TO GET MOST ANYTHING DONE IF IT BENEFITS NATIONAL SECURITY.
SO WHAT'LL IT BE?
IN OR OUT?
OPEN

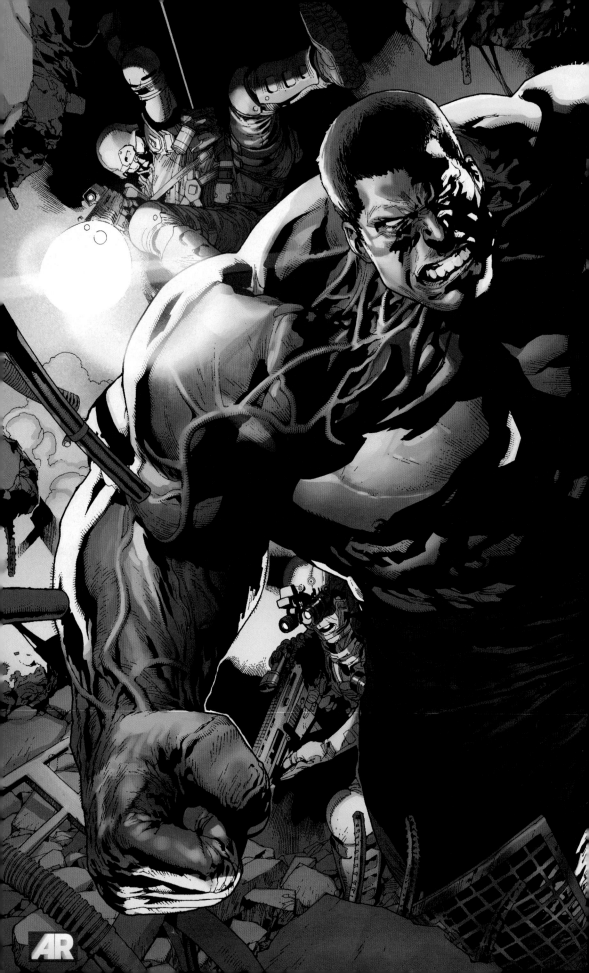

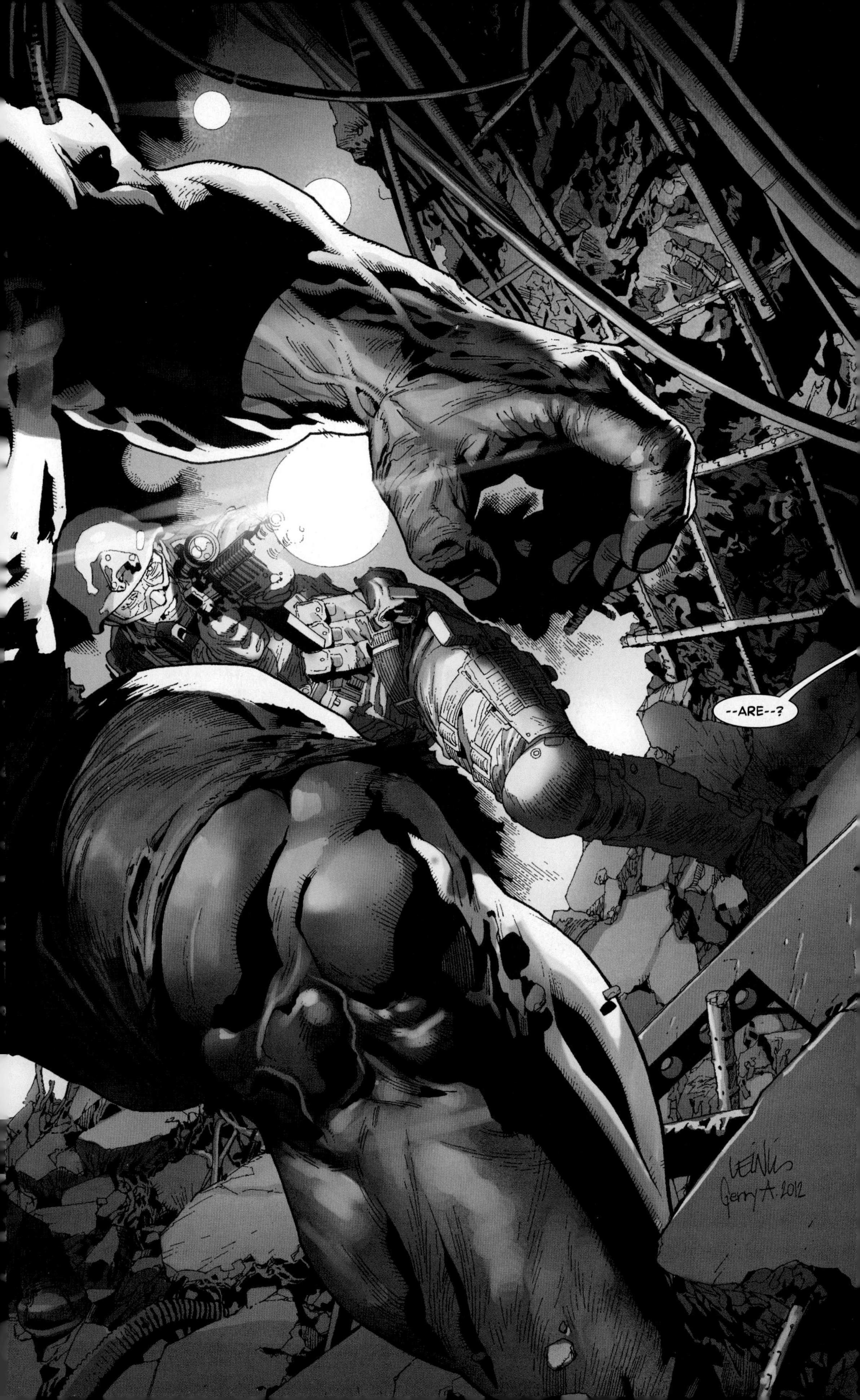
--ARE--?
Gerry A. 2012

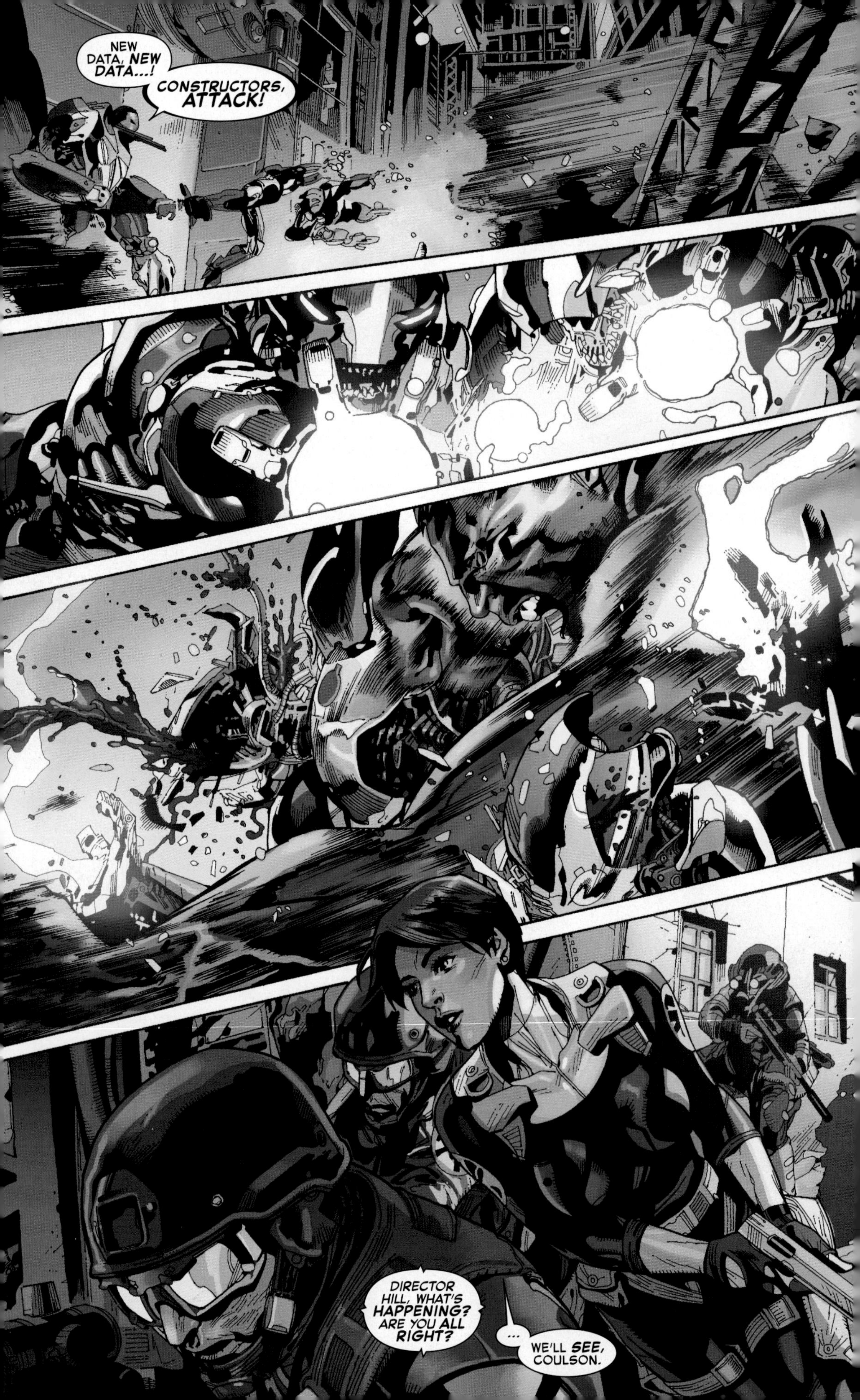
NEW DATA, NEW DATA...!
CONSTRUCTORS, ATTACK!
DIRECTOR HILL, WHAT'S HAPPENING? ARE YOU ALL RIGHT?
...
WE'LL SEE, COULSON.

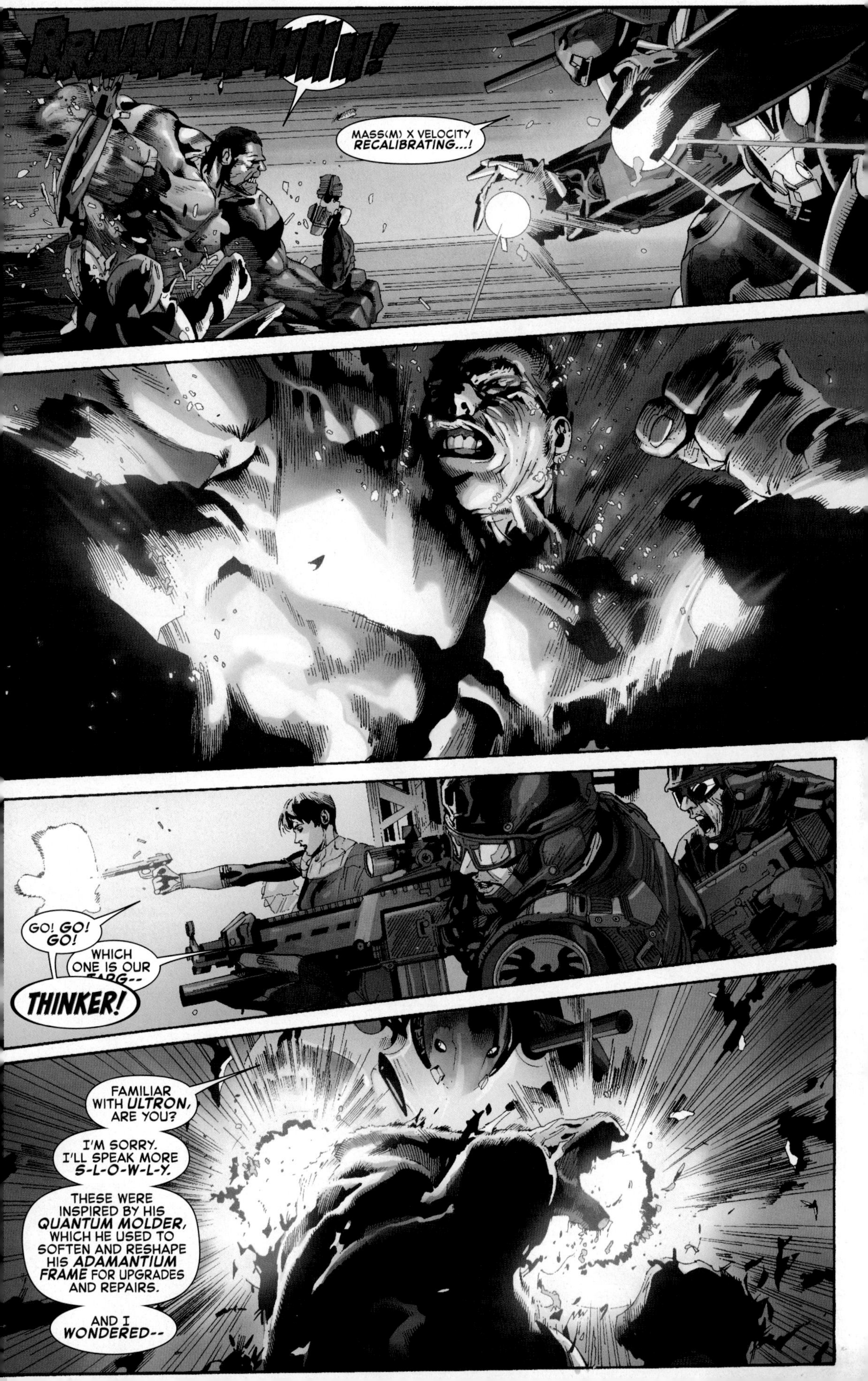
RRAAAAAAAHHH!
MASS(M) X VELOCITY RECALIBRATING...!
GO! GO! GO!
WHICH ONE IS OUR TARG--
THINKER!
FAMILIAR WITH ULTRON, ARE YOU?
I'M SORRY. I'LL SPEAK MORE S-L-O-W-L-Y.
THESE WERE INSPIRED BY HIS QUANTUM MOLDER, WHICH HE USED TO SOFTEN AND RESHAPE HIS ADAMANTIUM FRAME FOR UPGRADES AND REPAIRS.
AND I WONDERED--

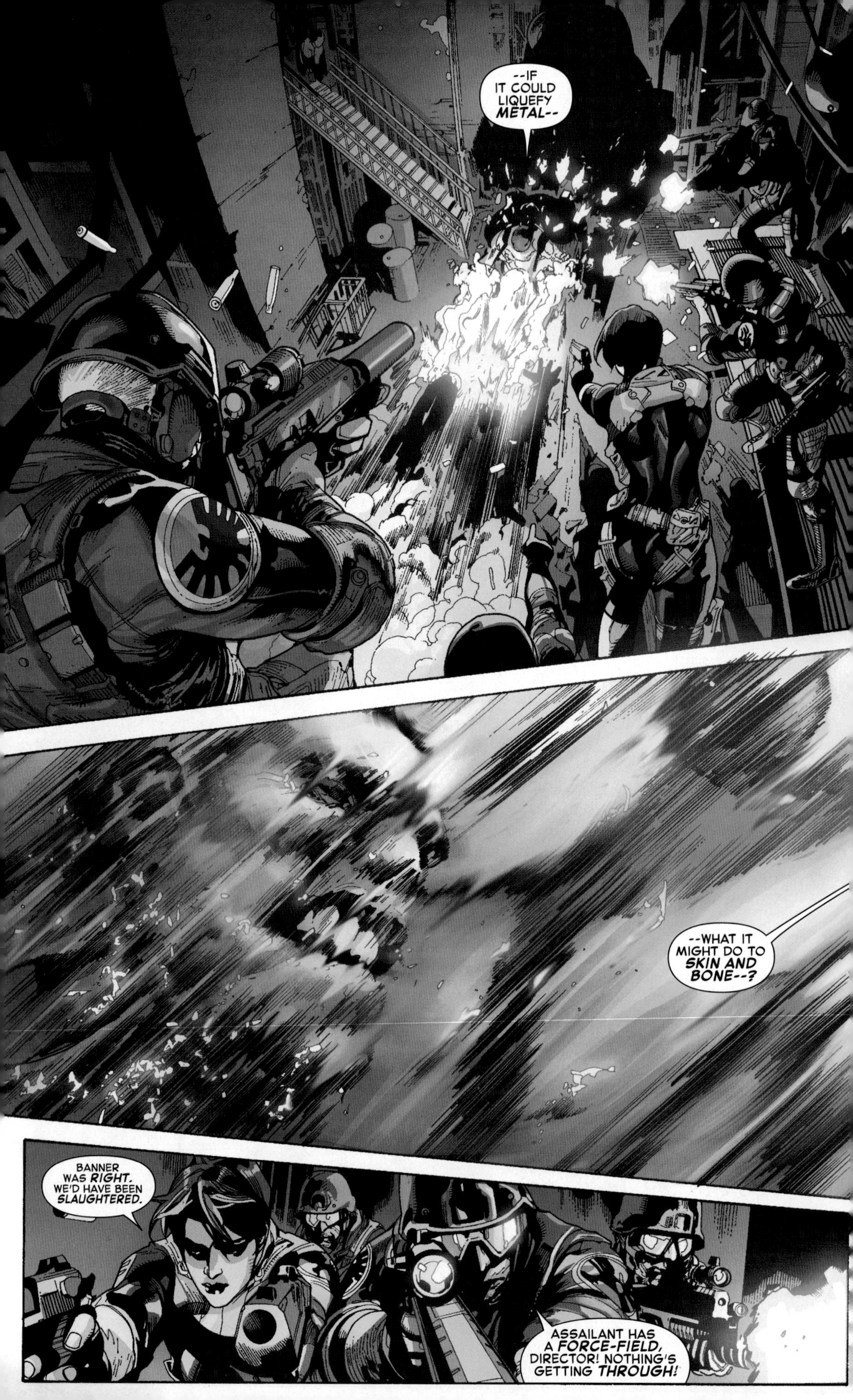
--IF IT COULD LIQUEFY METAL--
--WHAT IT MIGHT DO TO SKIN AND BONE--?
BANNER WAS RIGHT. WE'D HAVE BEEN SLAUGHTERED.
ASSAILANT HAS A FORCE-FIELD, DIRECTOR! NOTHING'S GETTING THROUGH!

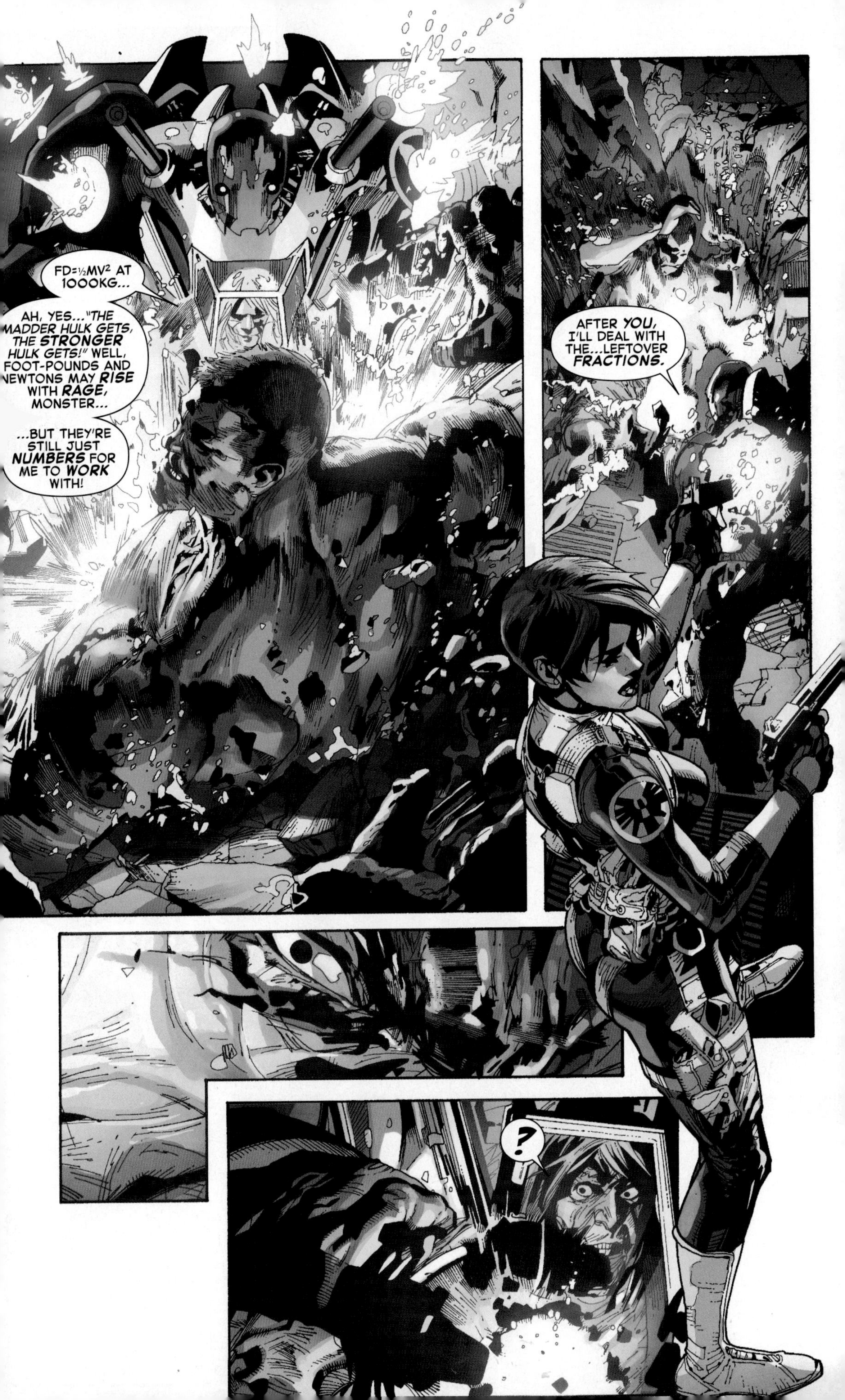
FD=½MV² AT 1000KG...
AH, YES... "THE MADDER HULK GETS, THE STRONGER HULK GETS!" WELL, FOOT-POUNDS AND NEWTONS MAY RISE WITH RAGE, MONSTER...
...BUT THEY'RE STILL JUST NUMBERS FOR ME TO WORK WITH!
AFTER YOU, I'LL DEAL WITH THE...LEFTOVER FRACTIONS.
?

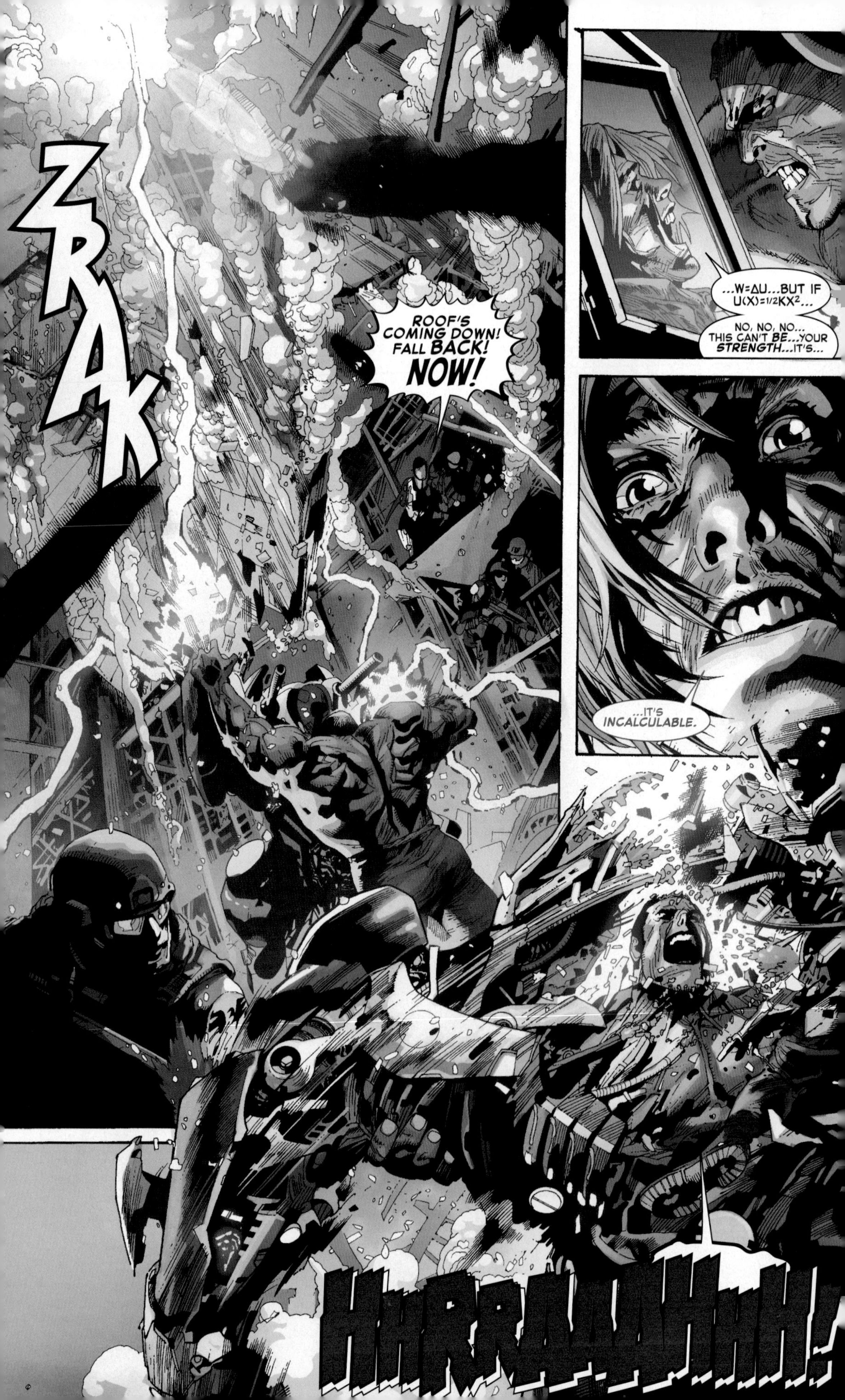
ZRAK
ROOF'S COMING DOWN! FALL BACK! NOW!
...$W=\Delta U$...BUT IF $U(X)=1/2KX^2$...
NO, NO, NO... THIS CAN'T BE...YOUR STRENGTH...IT'S...
...IT'S INCALCULABLE.
HHRAAAHHH!

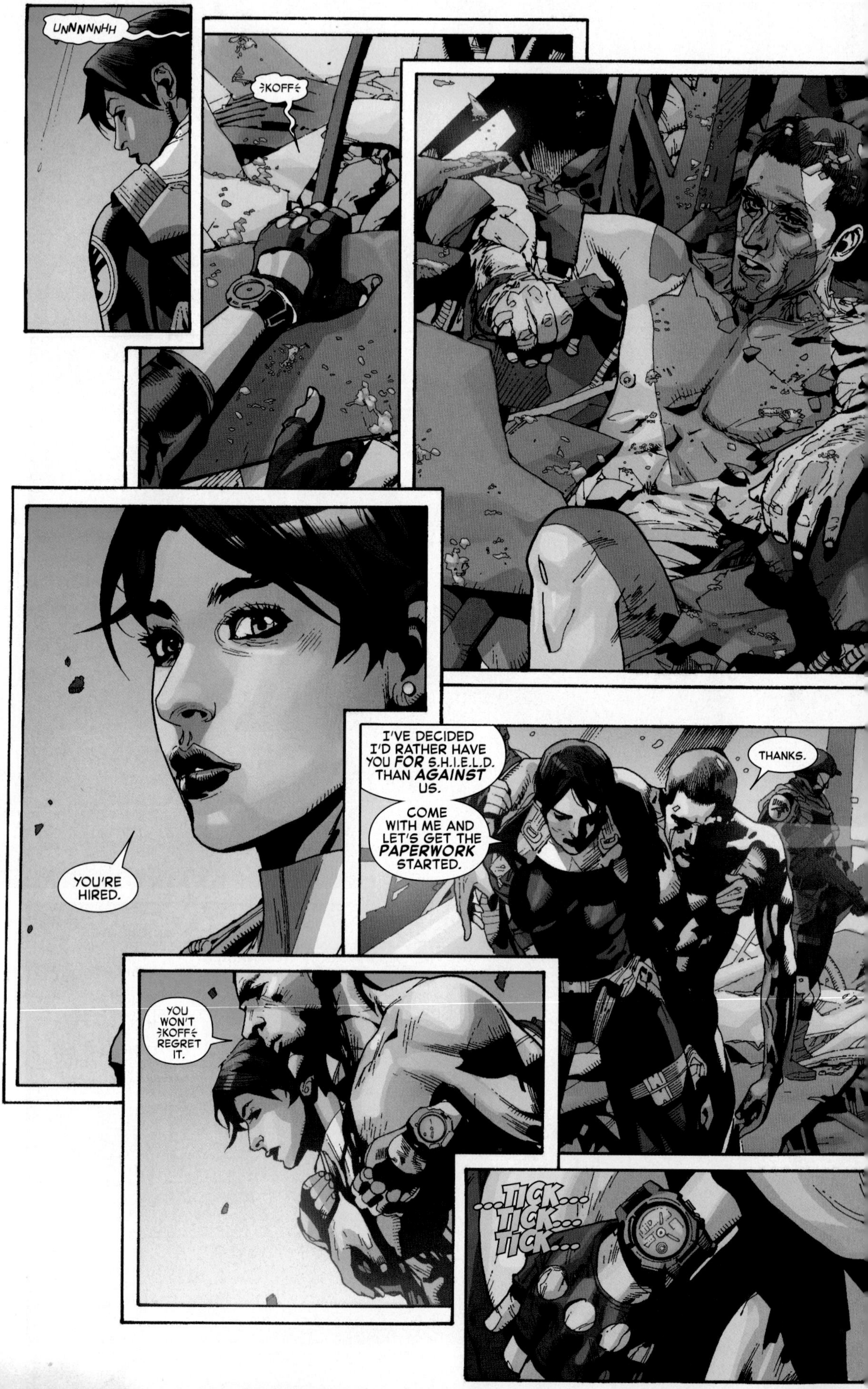
UNNNNNHH
≷KOFF≶
I'VE DECIDED I'D RATHER HAVE YOU FOR S.H.I.E.L.D. THAN AGAINST US.
COME WITH ME AND LET'S GET THE PAPERWORK STARTED.
THANKS.
YOU'RE HIRED.
YOU WON'T ≷KOFF≶ REGRET IT.
...TICK... TICK... TICK...

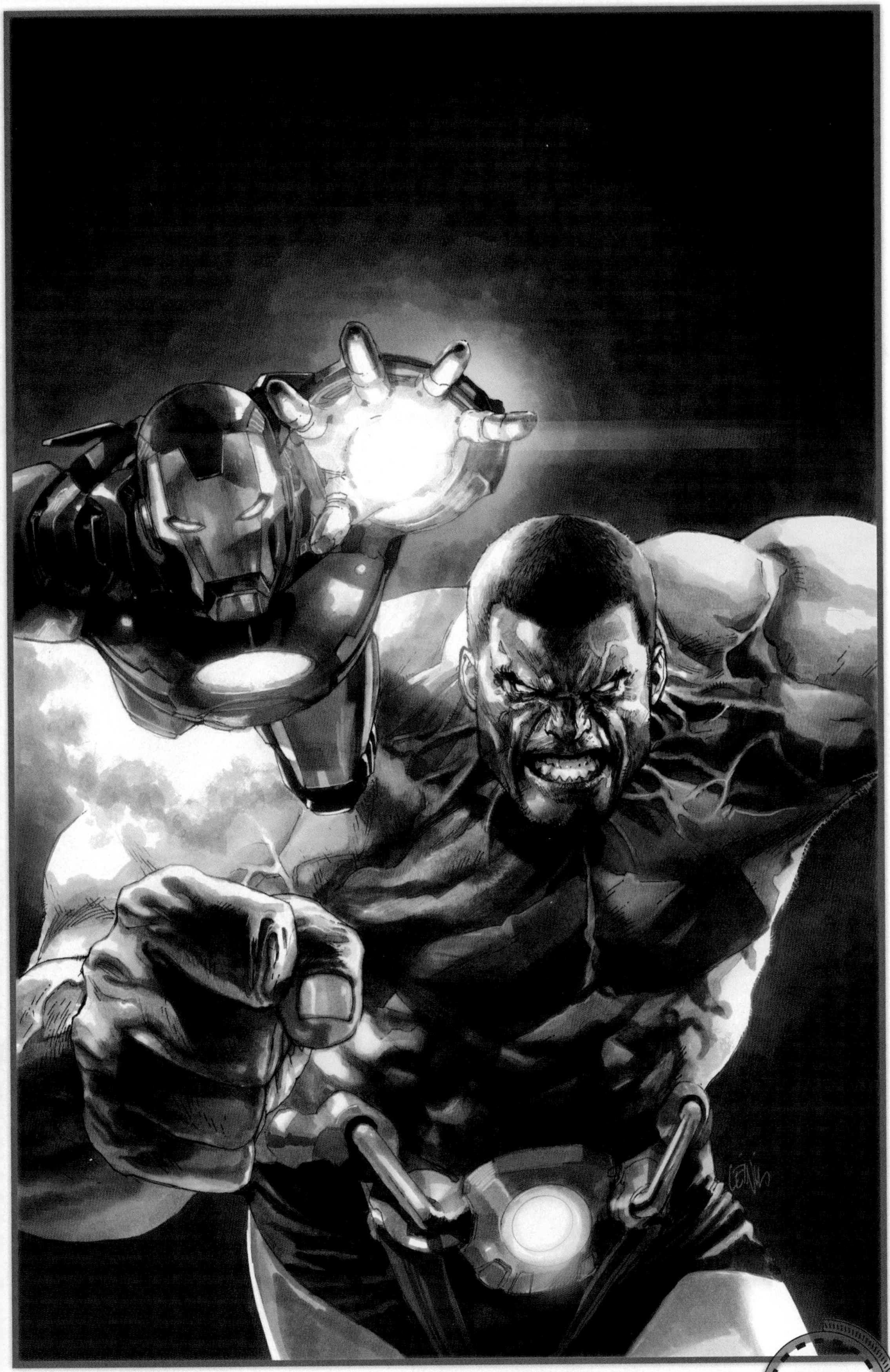

02

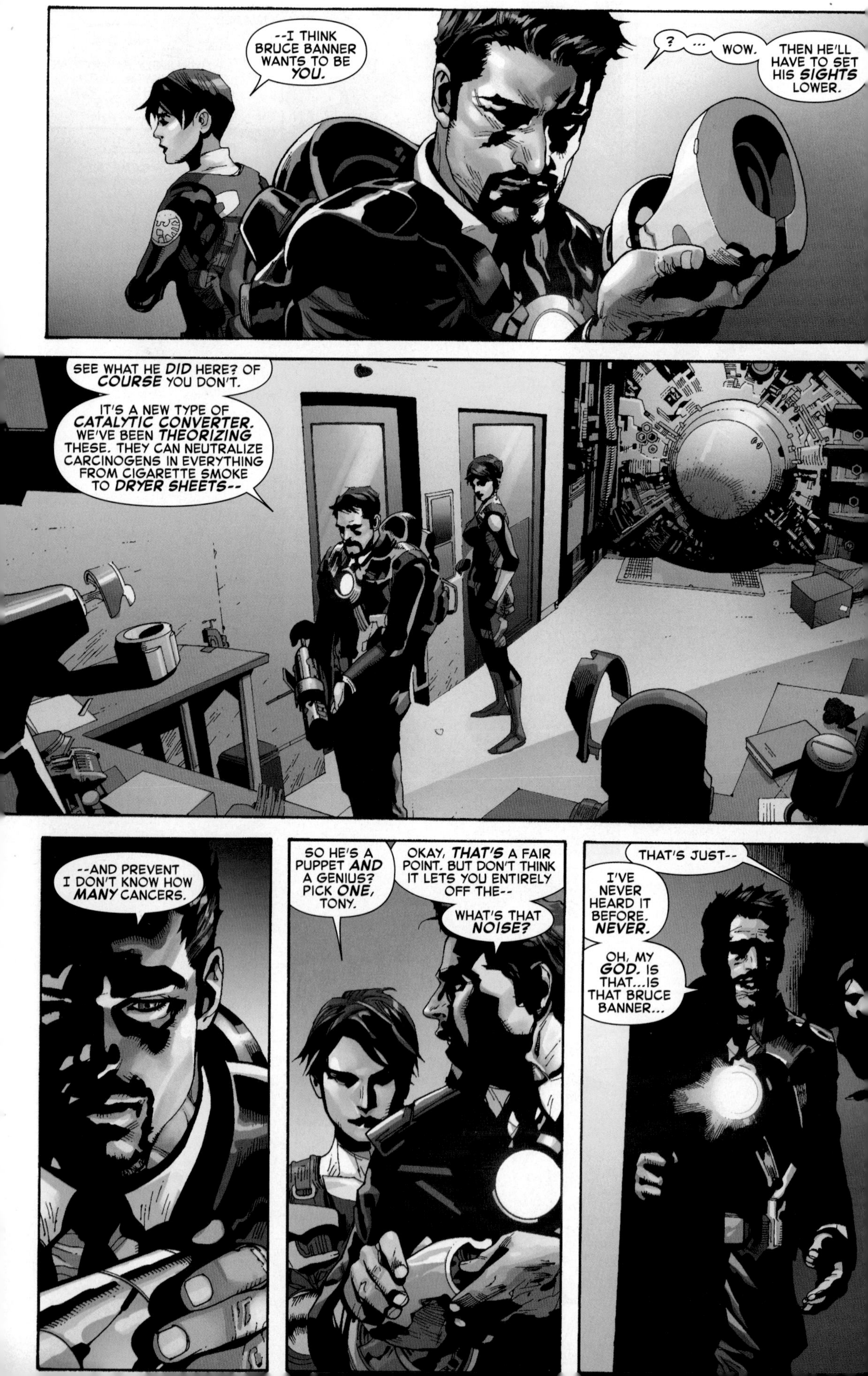

--I THINK BRUCE BANNER WANTS TO BE YOU.
? ...
WOW.
THEN HE'LL HAVE TO SET HIS SIGHTS LOWER.
SEE WHAT HE DID HERE? OF COURSE YOU DON'T.
IT'S A NEW TYPE OF CATALYTIC CONVERTER. WE'VE BEEN THEORIZING THESE. THEY CAN NEUTRALIZE CARCINOGENS IN EVERYTHING FROM CIGARETTE SMOKE TO DRYER SHEETS--
--AND PREVENT I DON'T KNOW HOW MANY CANCERS.
SO HE'S A PUPPET AND A GENIUS? PICK ONE, TONY.
OKAY, THAT'S A FAIR POINT. BUT DON'T THINK IT LETS YOU ENTIRELY OFF THE--
WHAT'S THAT NOISE?
THAT'S JUST--
I'VE NEVER HEARD IT BEFORE. NEVER.
OH, MY GOD. IS THAT...IS THAT BRUCE BANNER...

...LAUGHING?

AH HA HA HA HA!

OKAY, *MY* BANNER'S EMOTIONS RUN EXACTLY *THIS* GAMUT: HANGDOG TO *SUICIDAL!* MAKE HIM *HUMORLESS* AGAIN, THIS *MINUTE!*

...HEH HEH *TONY?* HEE HEH...

LOOK! IT'S *HILARIOUS!*

EVIDENTLY.

NO, *LOOK!*

SEE? IT'S A *PUN!*

OH. OH!

I *KNOW,* RIGHT?

WHAT?

YOU WOULDN'T GET IT.

⇒SIGH⇐

HAHAHAHAHAHAHAHAHAHA

⇒SNIF⇐

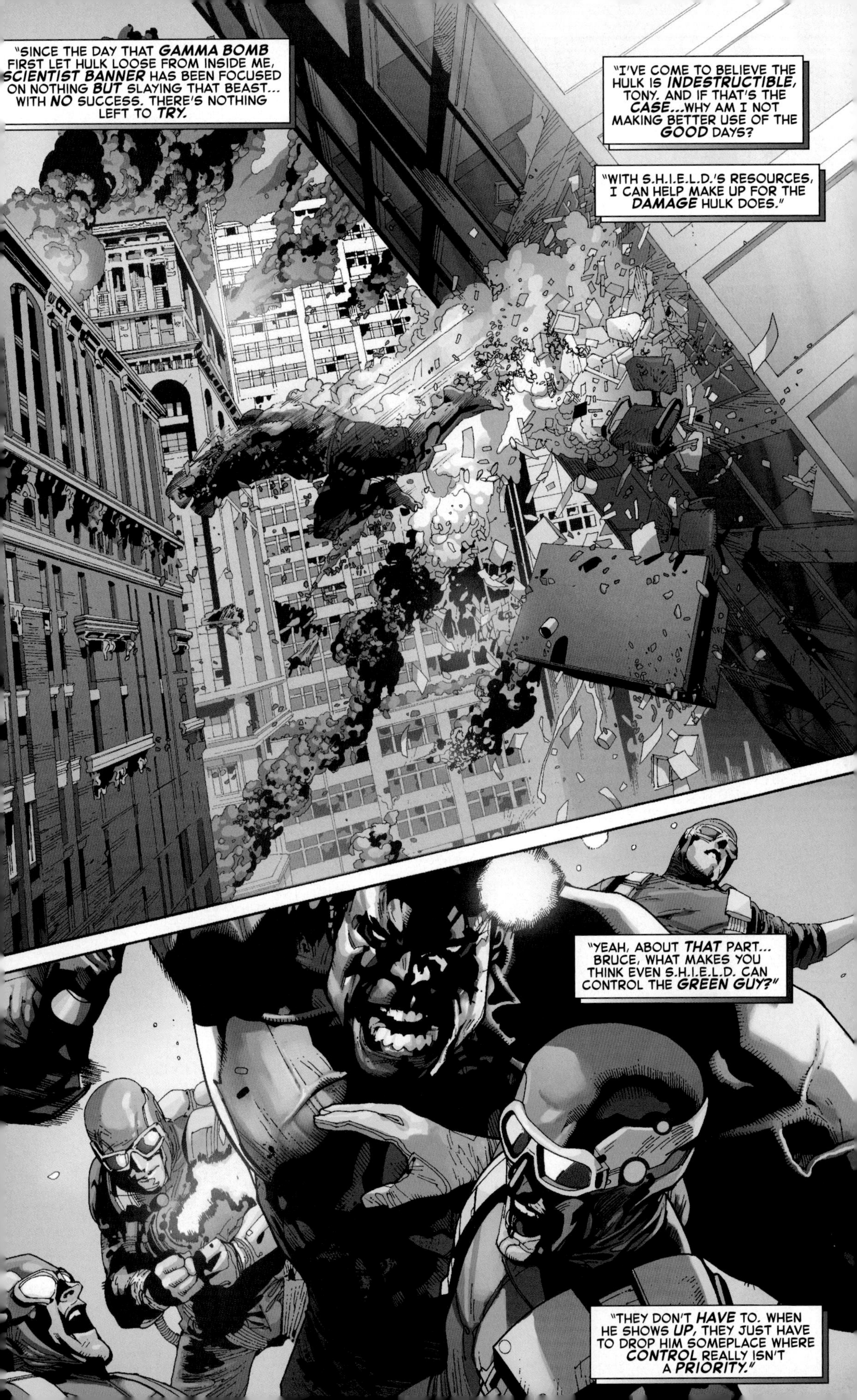
"SINCE THE DAY THAT GAMMA BOMB FIRST LET HULK LOOSE FROM INSIDE ME, SCIENTIST BANNER HAS BEEN FOCUSED ON NOTHING BUT SLAYING THAT BEAST... WITH NO SUCCESS. THERE'S NOTHING LEFT TO TRY.
"I'VE COME TO BELIEVE THE HULK IS INDESTRUCTIBLE, TONY. AND IF THAT'S THE CASE...WHY AM I NOT MAKING BETTER USE OF THE GOOD DAYS?
"WITH S.H.I.E.L.D.'S RESOURCES, I CAN HELP MAKE UP FOR THE DAMAGE HULK DOES."
"YEAH, ABOUT THAT PART... BRUCE, WHAT MAKES YOU THINK EVEN S.H.I.E.L.D. CAN CONTROL THE GREEN GUY?"
"THEY DON'T HAVE TO. WHEN HE SHOWS UP, THEY JUST HAVE TO DROP HIM SOMEPLACE WHERE CONTROL REALLY ISN'T A PRIORITY."

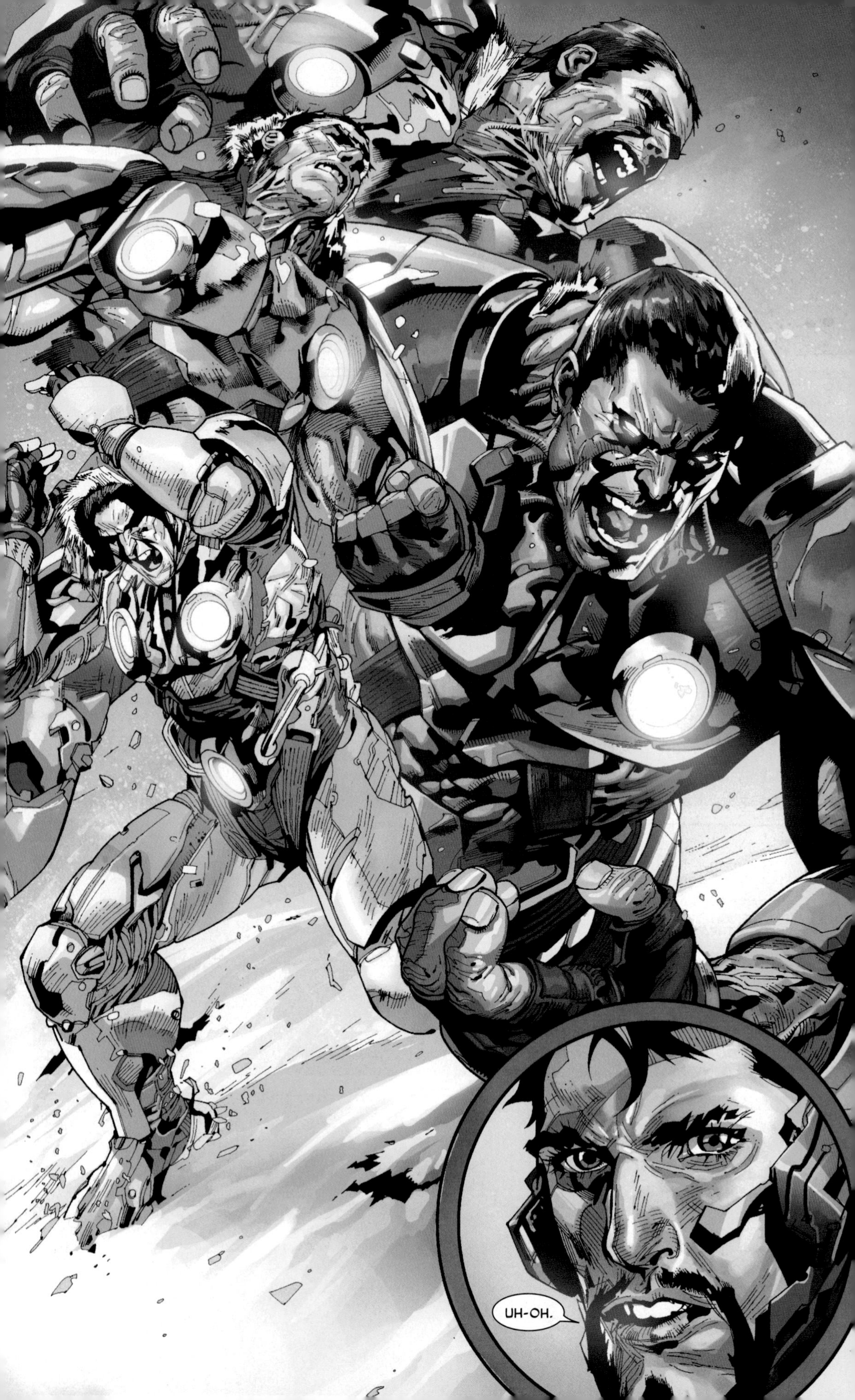
UH-OH.

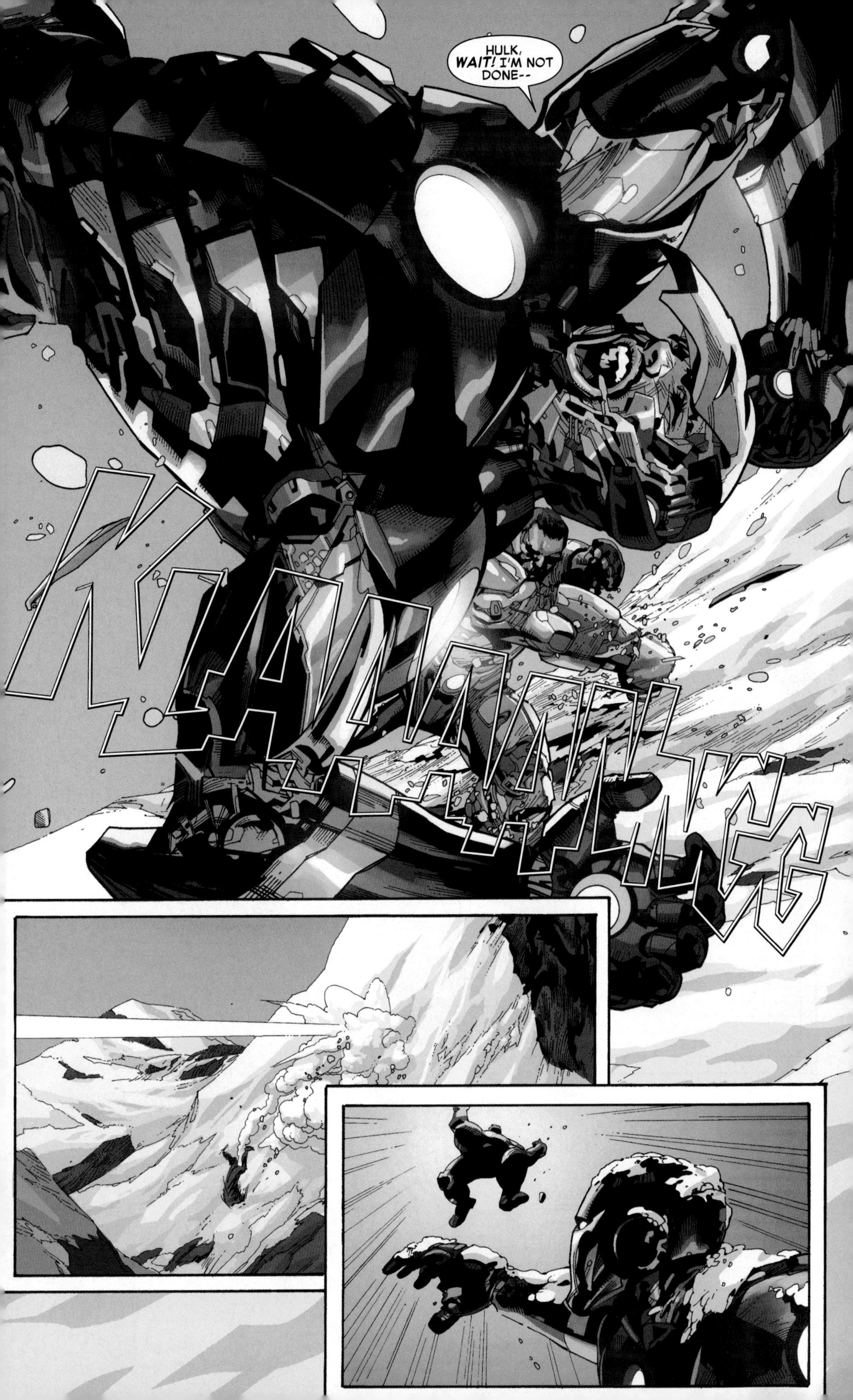
HULK, WAIT! I'M NOT DONE--
KWAAAANNNNGG

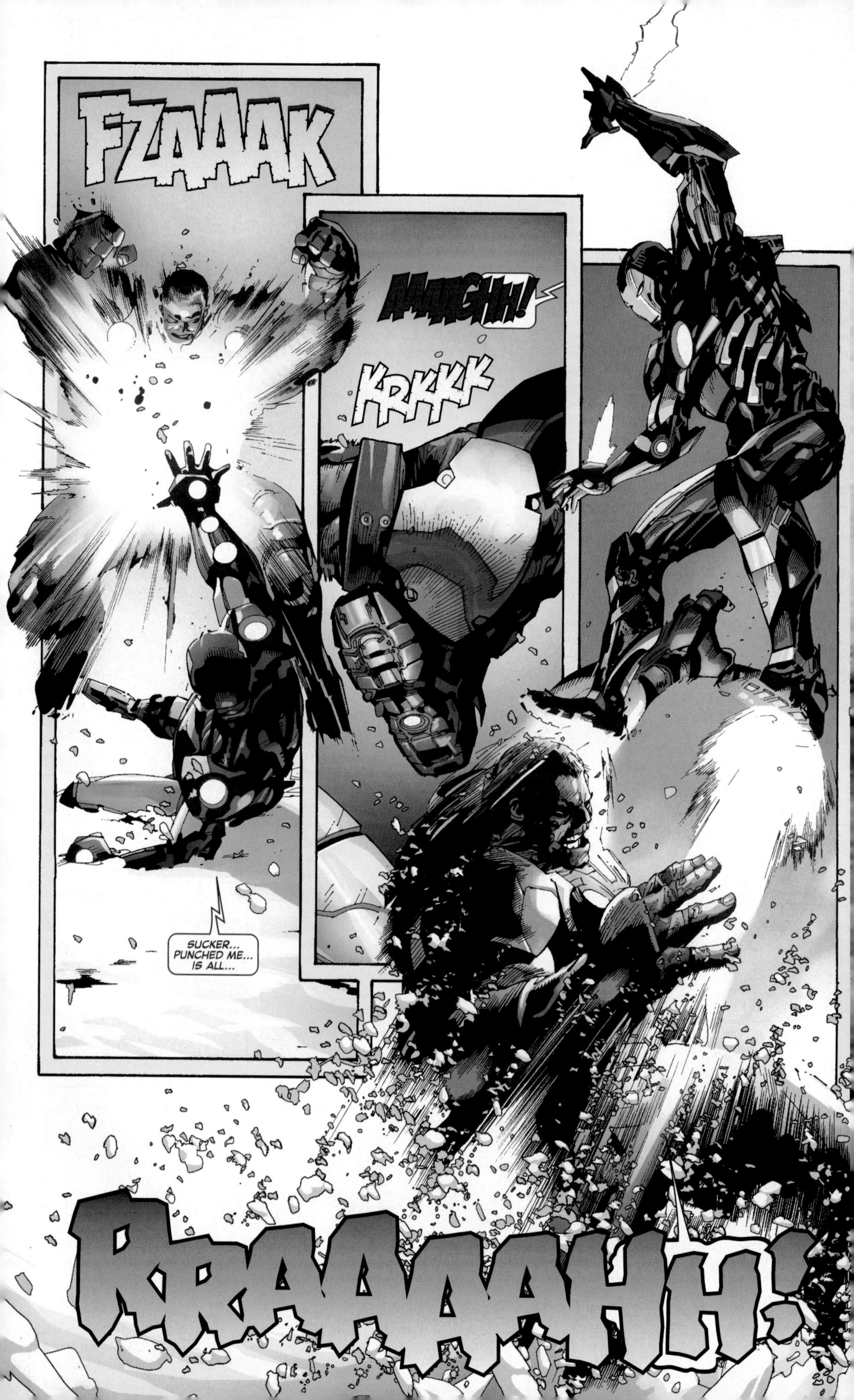
FZAAAK
AAAAGHH!
KRKKK
SUCKER... PUNCHED ME... IS ALL...
RRAAAAHH!

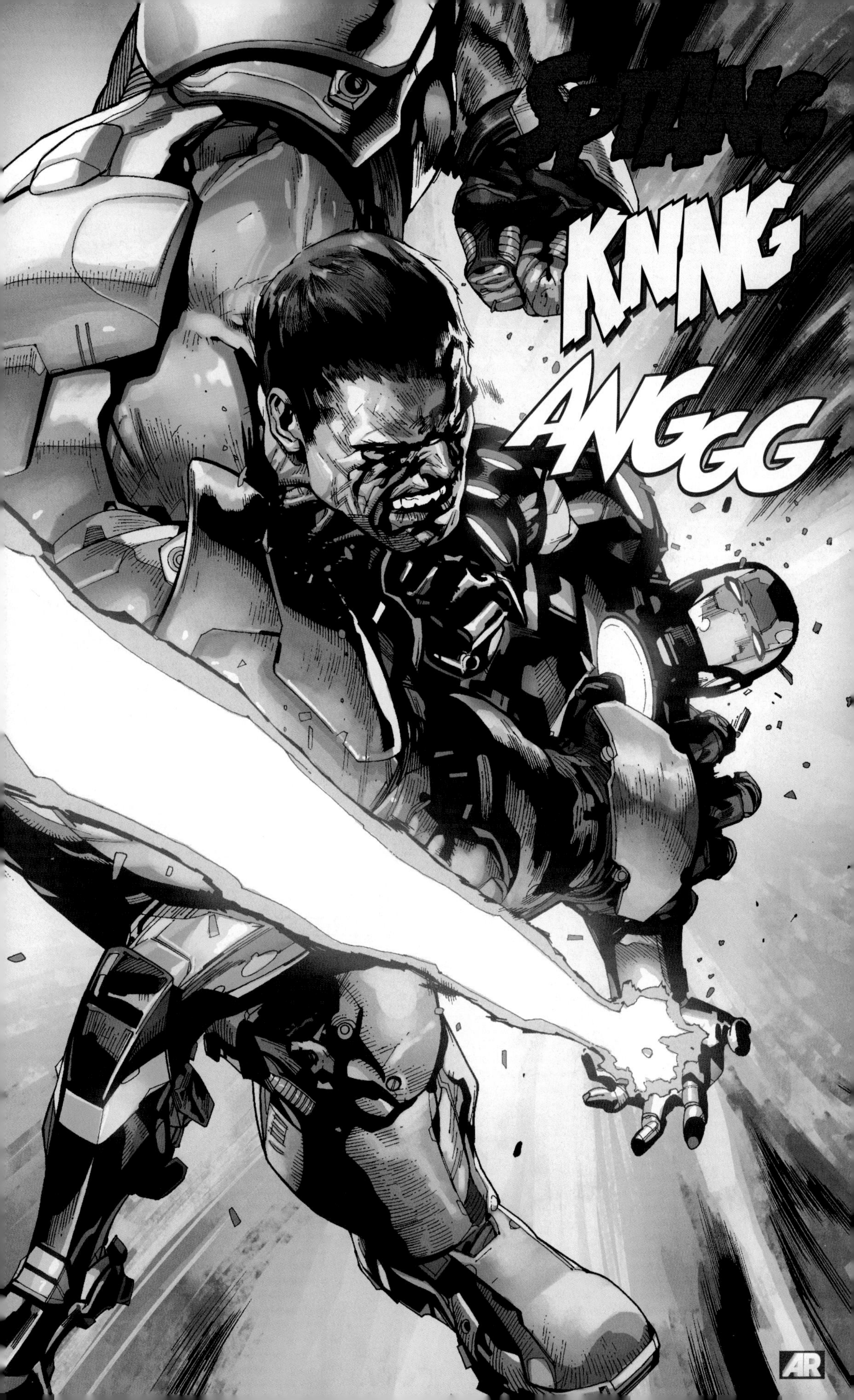
KNNG
ANGGG

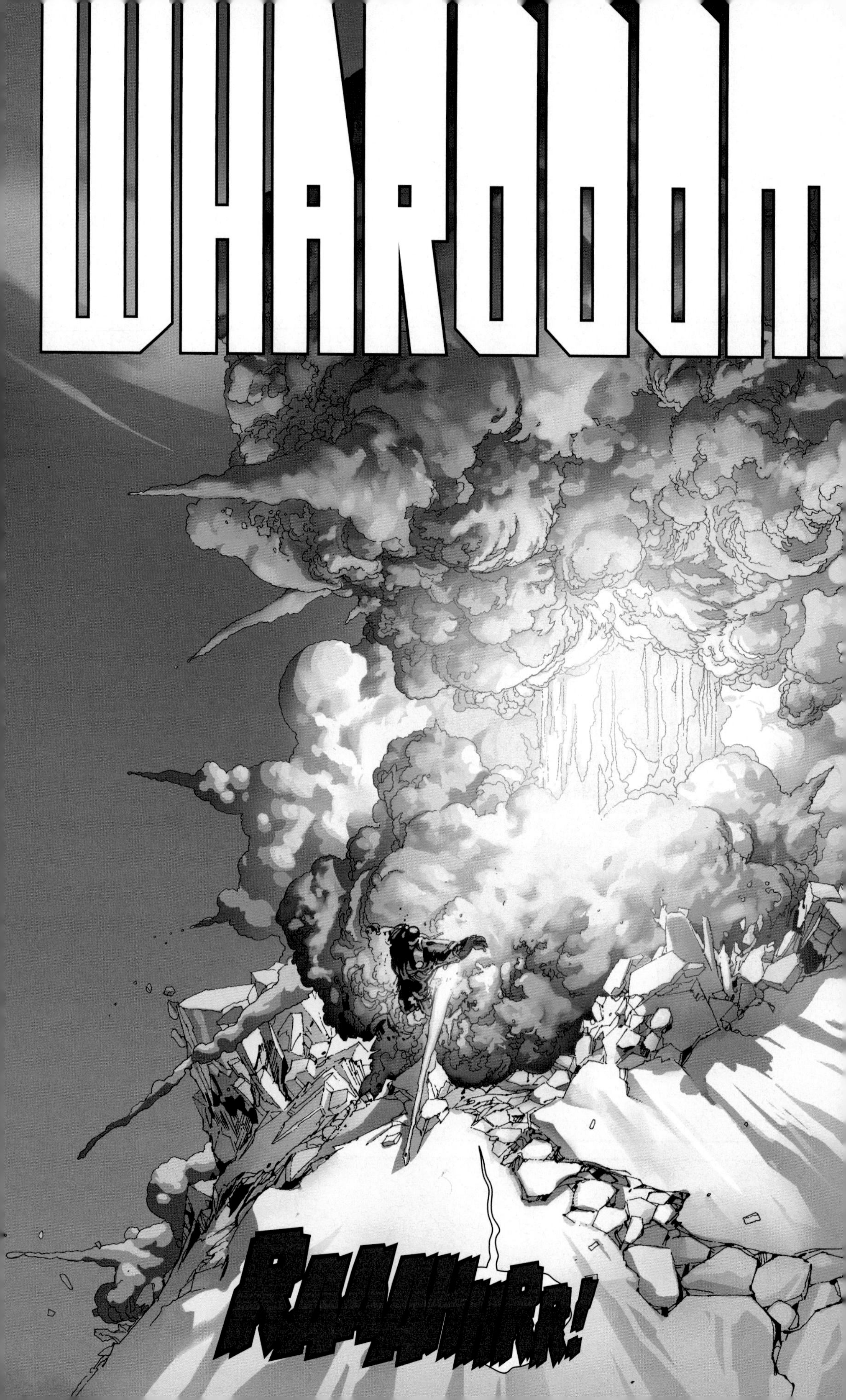
WHAROOM
RAAAHHRR!

NNUUHHHH...

YOU... YOU SAVED ME...

WHAT...

...WHAT'D I MISS...?

I THINK YOUR GIZMO ATE A MOUNTAIN.

I COULD EAT A MOUNTAIN.

...AND ONCE YOU GET YOUR *STAFF* IN PLACE, CALL ON ME *ANYTIME.* I CAN SHARE WHAT I KNOW ABOUT MANAGEMENT...

...WORKER SAFETY...E.P.A. REGS...

I STILL CAN'T *GET OVER* WHAT *MARIA* SAID TO YOU.

IT'S NOT SO CRAZY.

PLEASE. I WANT TO BE *YOU?* OLD-SCHOOL *YOU?* NEWTONIAN, ARCHIMEDEAN, *"OOOH! NANITES!"* YOU?

YOU'RE A *BRILLIANT ENGINEER,* TONY--BUT ALL *YOU* EVER DO IS BUILD *FORWARD* FROM WHAT YOU ALREADY *KNOW.*

A *TRUE* VISIONARY STUDIES THE *UNKNOWN* AND BUILDS *BACKWARD.* IT'S A *NEW FIELD*--

--AND A *LEGITIMATE* ONE. THE NOVELIST CHARLES YU CALLS IT *"APPLIED SCIENCE FICTION."*

I'M SORRY, AM I *INTIMIDATING* YOU?

YOU? PLEASE.

EXCUSE ME A MINUTE.

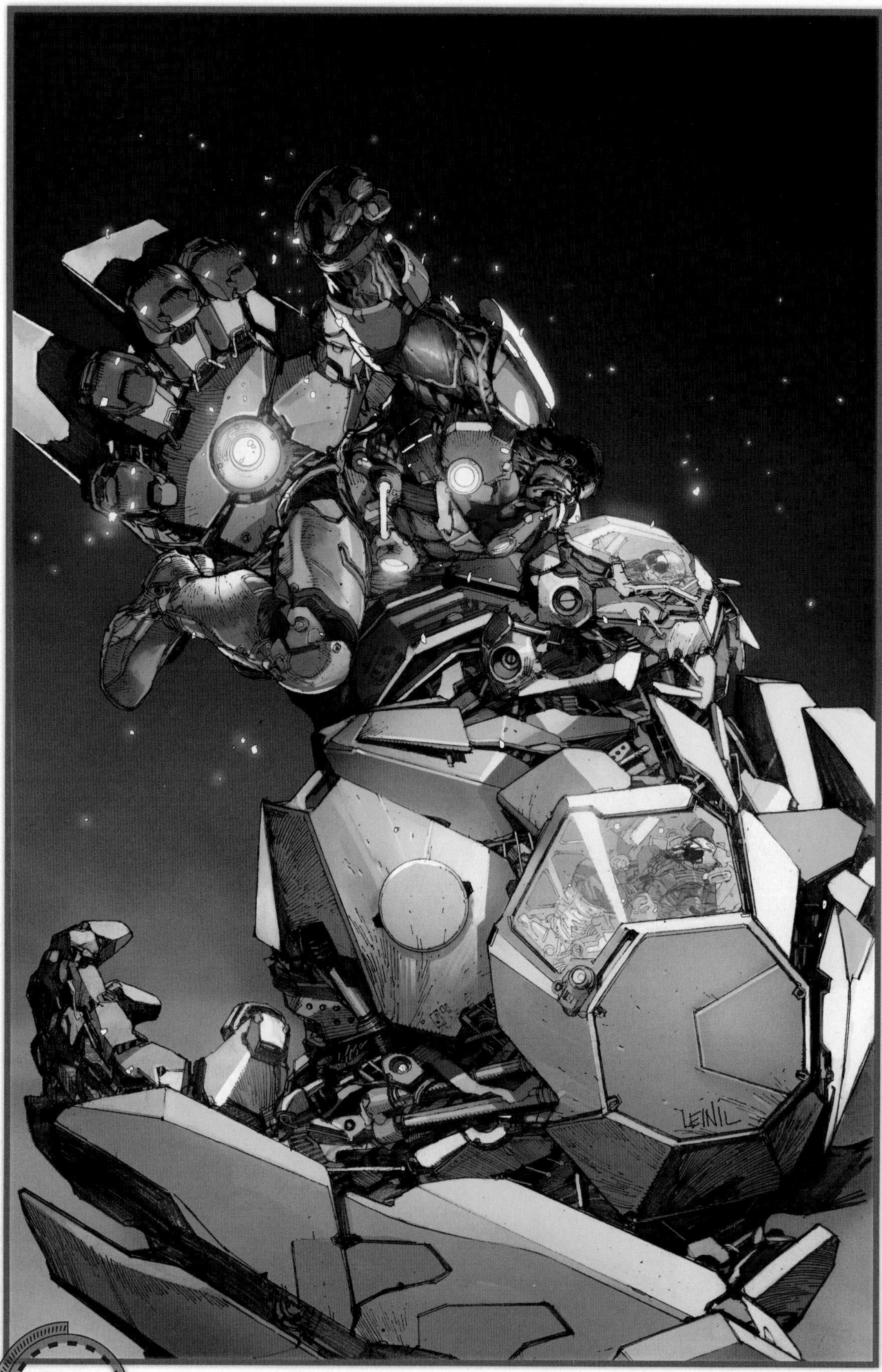
LEINIL

03

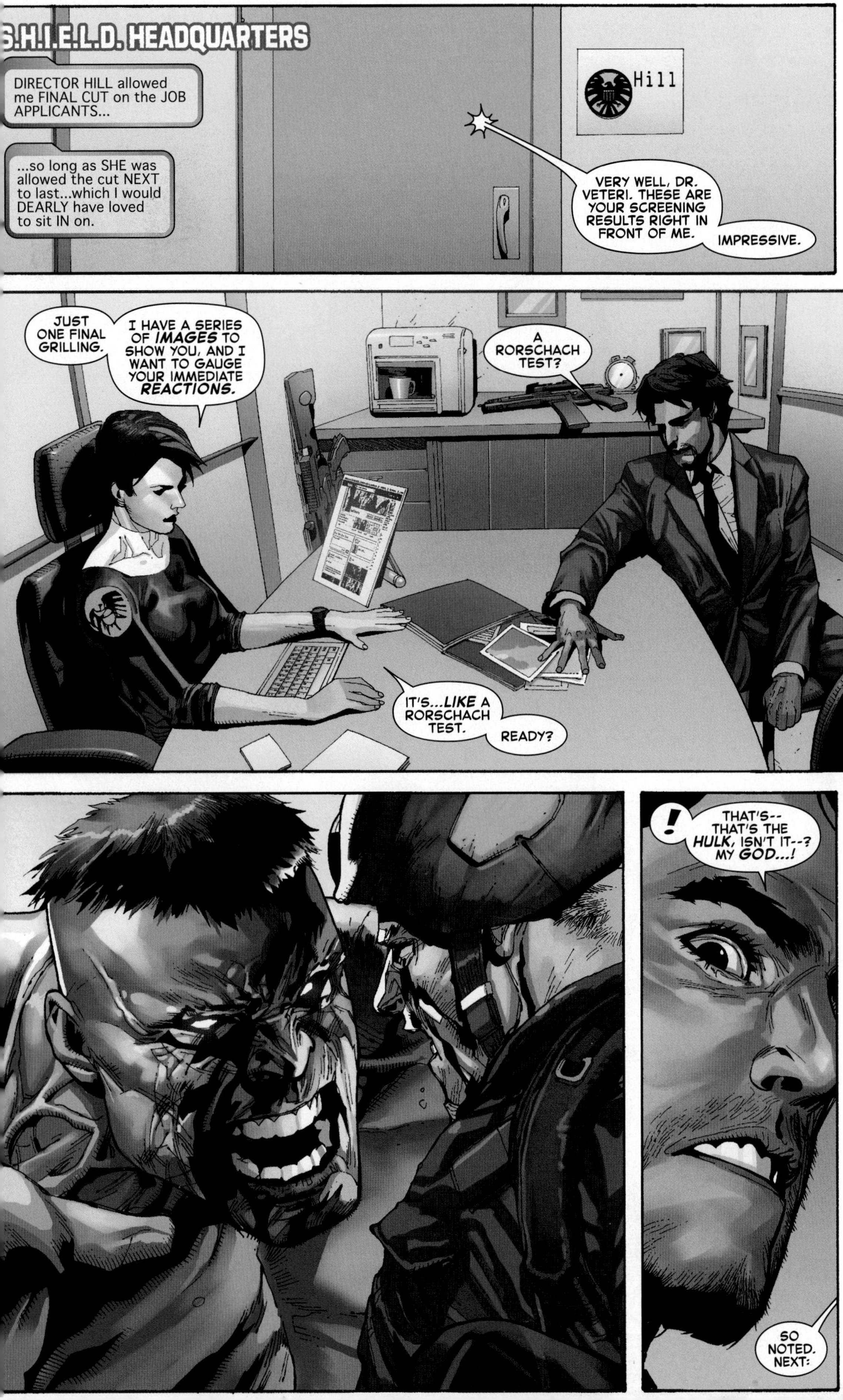
S.H.I.E.L.D. HEADQUARTERS
DIRECTOR HILL allowed me FINAL CUT on the JOB APPLICANTS...
...so long as SHE was allowed the cut NEXT to last...which I would DEARLY have loved to sit IN on.
Hill
VERY WELL, DR. VETERI. THESE ARE YOUR SCREENING RESULTS RIGHT IN FRONT OF ME.
IMPRESSIVE.
JUST ONE FINAL GRILLING.
I HAVE A SERIES OF IMAGES TO SHOW YOU, AND I WANT TO GAUGE YOUR IMMEDIATE REACTIONS.
A RORSCHACH TEST?
IT'S...LIKE A RORSCHACH TEST.
READY?
!
THAT'S--THAT'S THE HULK, ISN'T IT--? MY GOD...!
SO NOTED. NEXT:

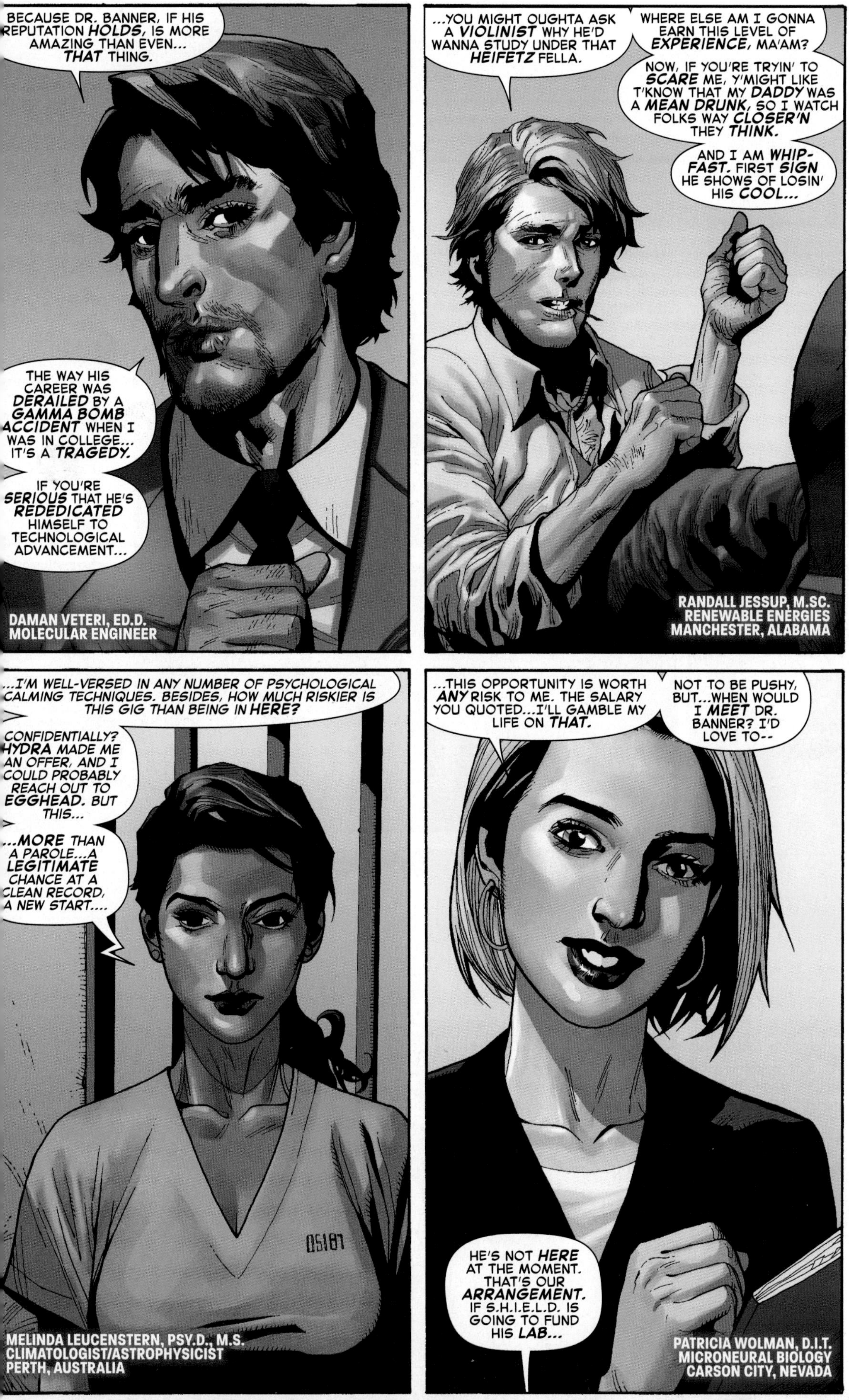
BECAUSE DR. BANNER, IF HIS REPUTATION HOLDS, IS MORE AMAZING THAN EVEN... THAT THING.
THE WAY HIS CAREER WAS DERAILED BY A GAMMA BOMB ACCIDENT WHEN I WAS IN COLLEGE... IT'S A TRAGEDY.
IF YOU'RE SERIOUS THAT HE'S REDEDICATED HIMSELF TO TECHNOLOGICAL ADVANCEMENT...
DAMAN VETERI, ED.D.
MOLECULAR ENGINEER
...YOU MIGHT OUGHTA ASK A VIOLINIST WHY HE'D WANNA STUDY UNDER THAT HEIFETZ FELLA.
WHERE ELSE AM I GONNA EARN THIS LEVEL OF EXPERIENCE, MA'AM?
NOW, IF YOU'RE TRYIN' TO SCARE ME, Y'MIGHT LIKE T'KNOW THAT MY DADDY WAS A MEAN DRUNK, SO I WATCH FOLKS WAY CLOSER'N THEY THINK.
AND I AM WHIP-FAST. FIRST SIGN HE SHOWS OF LOSIN' HIS COOL...
RANDALL JESSUP, M.SC.
RENEWABLE ENERGIES
MANCHESTER, ALABAMA
...I'M WELL-VERSED IN ANY NUMBER OF PSYCHOLOGICAL CALMING TECHNIQUES. BESIDES, HOW MUCH RISKIER IS THIS GIG THAN BEING IN HERE?
CONFIDENTIALLY? HYDRA MADE ME AN OFFER, AND I COULD PROBABLY REACH OUT TO EGGHEAD. BUT THIS...
...MORE THAN A PAROLE...A LEGITIMATE CHANCE AT A CLEAN RECORD, A NEW START....
05187
MELINDA LEUCENSTERN, PSY.D., M.S.
CLIMATOLOGIST/ASTROPHYSICIST
PERTH, AUSTRALIA
...THIS OPPORTUNITY IS WORTH ANY RISK TO ME. THE SALARY YOU QUOTED...I'LL GAMBLE MY LIFE ON THAT.
NOT TO BE PUSHY, BUT...WHEN WOULD I MEET DR. BANNER? I'D LOVE TO--
HE'S NOT HERE AT THE MOMENT. THAT'S OUR ARRANGEMENT. IF S.H.I.E.L.D. IS GOING TO FUND HIS LAB...
PATRICIA WOLMAN, D.I.T.
MICRONEURAL BIOLOGY
CARSON CITY, NEVADA

"...HE HAS TO DO US A *FAVOR* NOW AND THEN."

≷HFFF≷

OH, AND *ALSO*--

HULLO. WHAT CAN I *DO* FOR--

AFTER WE'VE GONE TO SO MUCH TROUBLE TO *FIND* YOU, *"MR. SMITH"?* OR, RATHER, *PROFESSOR BURKE?* YOU CAN LET US *IN.*

--YOU CAN WEAR *THIS.*

FINALLY, YOU CAN COME *WITH*--

SAVE YOUR BREATH. HE CAN'T HEAR YOU IN THAT THING.

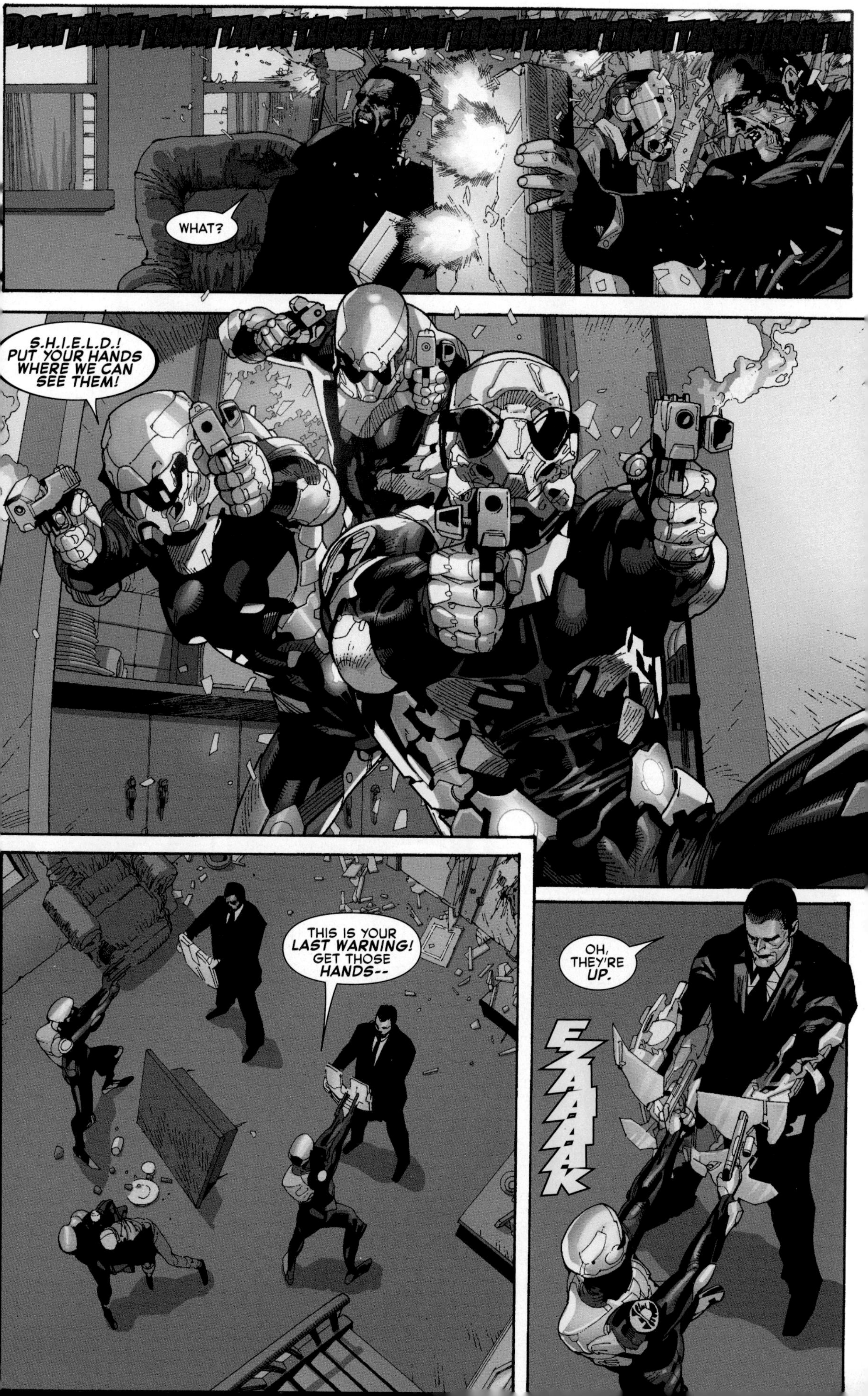
WHAT?
S.H.I.E.L.D.! PUT YOUR HANDS WHERE WE CAN SEE THEM!
THIS IS YOUR LAST WARNING! GET THOSE HANDS--
OH, THEY'RE UP.

DEVIL'S MOUTH, SOUTH PACIFIC

RESEARCH AND DEVELOPMENT SITE FOR
TECHNOLOGICAL TERRORIST GROUP A.I.M.

I WAS *APPRISED* AS TO YOUR LITTLE *ACTION SCENE.* WE'LL BE *LUCKY* IF YOU WEREN'T *TAILED.*

SHUT *UP.* HOW HAS THIS PROFESSION BECOME SO *DEBASED?*

WHAT YOU CALL *ESPIONAGE,* WE USED TO CALL *FAILURE.* NOW IT'S ALL CONSPICUOUS *VIOLENCE,* EXPENSIVE *WEAPONRY*--

MR. THIRTY-THREE, SIR, THAT'S *IMPOSSI*--

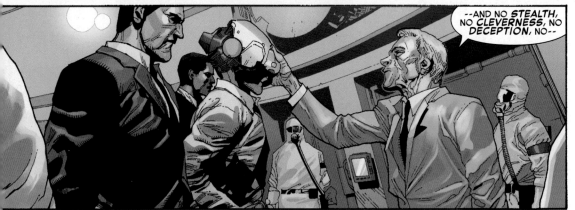

--AND NO *STEALTH,* NO *CLEVERNESS,* NO *DECEPTION,* NO--

WELL.

I STAND *CORRECTED.* THEY CALL ME *COLIN THIRTY-THREE,* SIR. AND WHO MIGHT *YOU* BE?

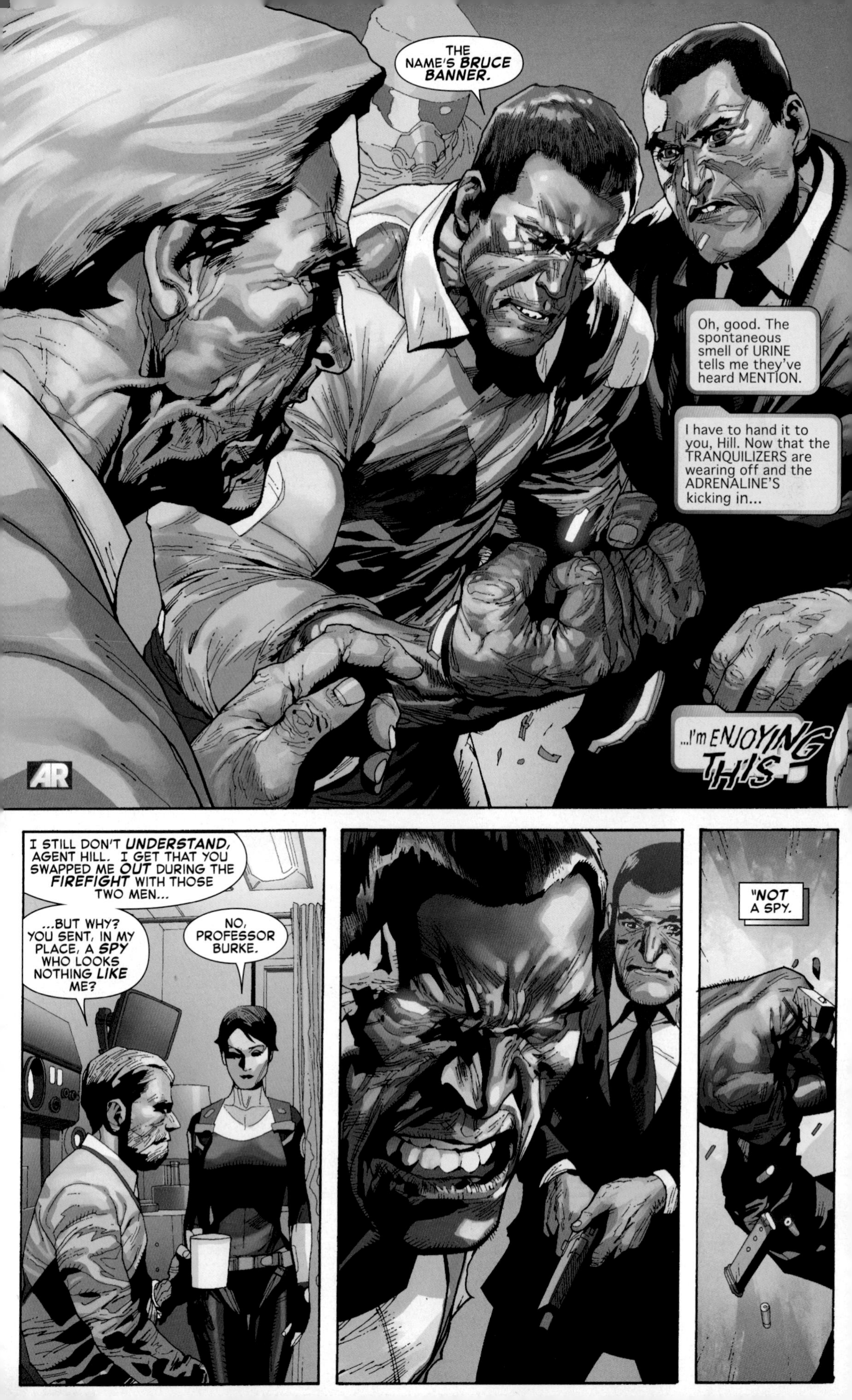
THE NAME'S BRUCE BANNER.
Oh, good. The spontaneous smell of URINE tells me they've heard MENTION.
I have to hand it to you, Hill. Now that the TRANQUILIZERS are wearing off and the ADRENALINE'S kicking in...
...I'm ENJOYING THIS.
I STILL DON'T UNDERSTAND, AGENT HILL. I GET THAT YOU SWAPPED ME OUT DURING THE FIREFIGHT WITH THOSE TWO MEN...
...BUT WHY? YOU SENT, IN MY PLACE, A SPY WHO LOOKS NOTHING LIKE ME?
NO, PROFESSOR BURKE.
"NOT A SPY.

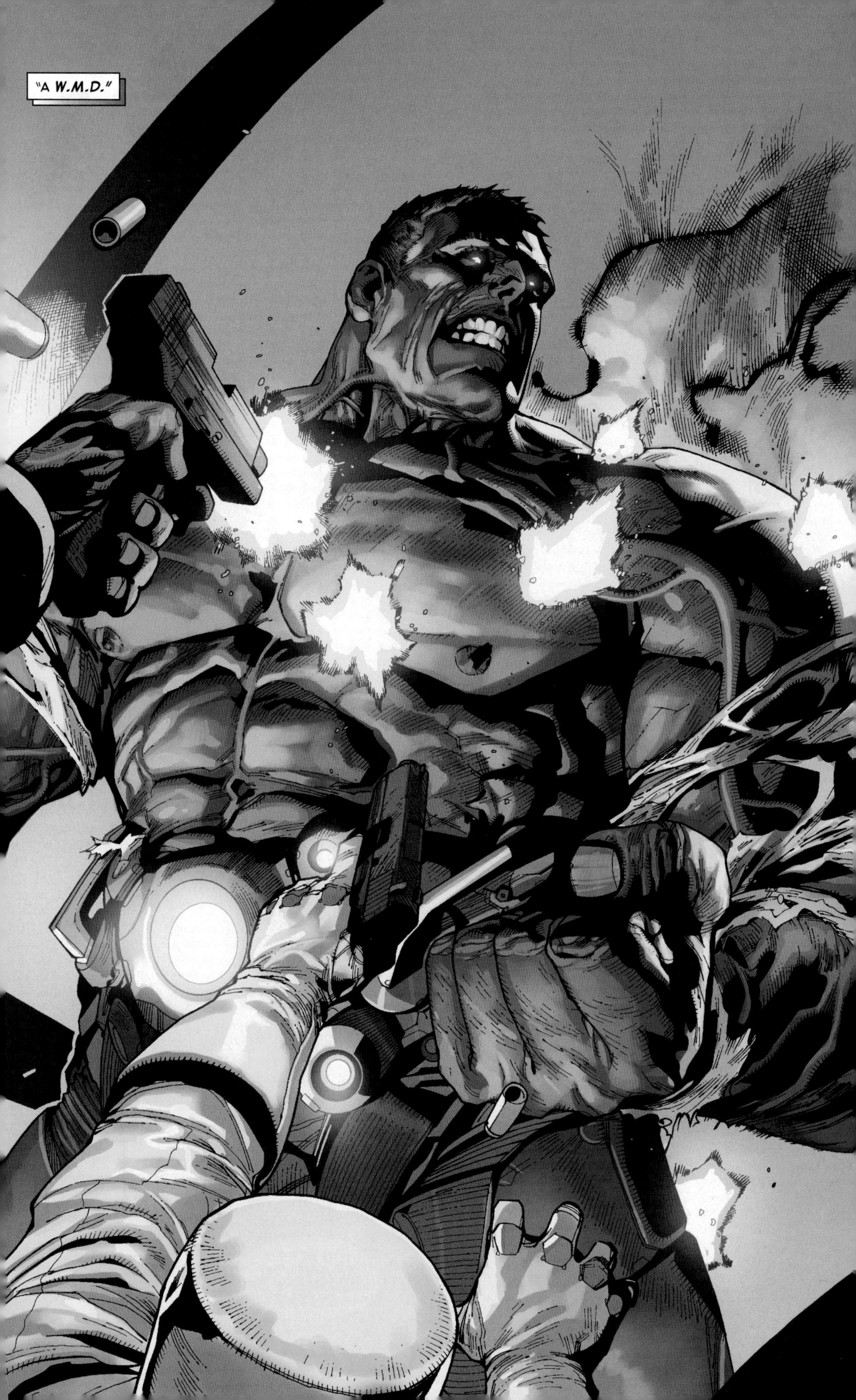
"A W.M.D."

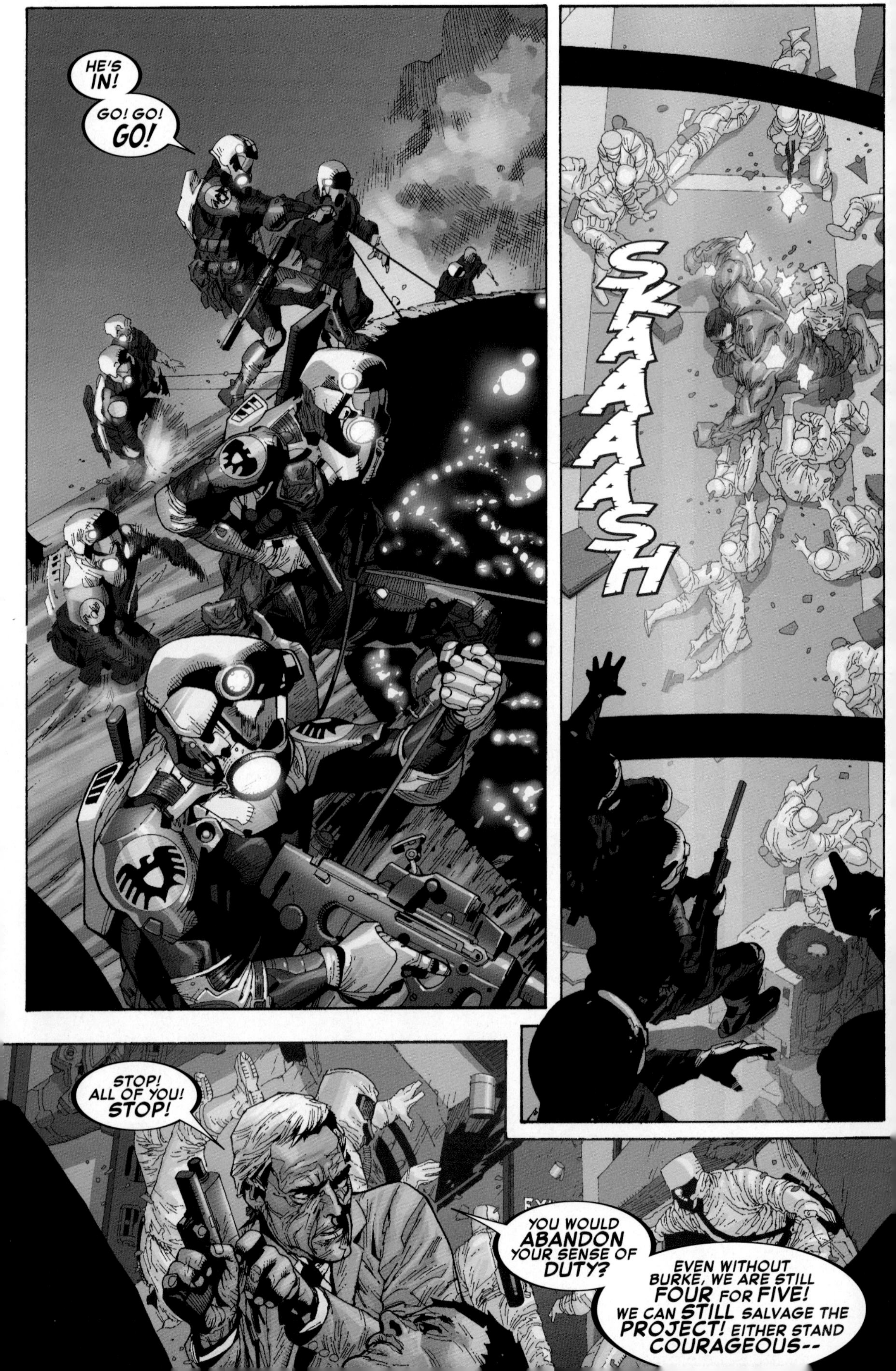
HE'S IN!
GO! GO! GO!
SKAAAAASH
STOP! ALL OF YOU! STOP!
YOU WOULD ABANDON YOUR SENSE OF DUTY?
EVEN WITHOUT BURKE, WE ARE STILL FOUR FOR FIVE! WE CAN STILL SALVAGE THE PROJECT! EITHER STAND COURAGEOUS--

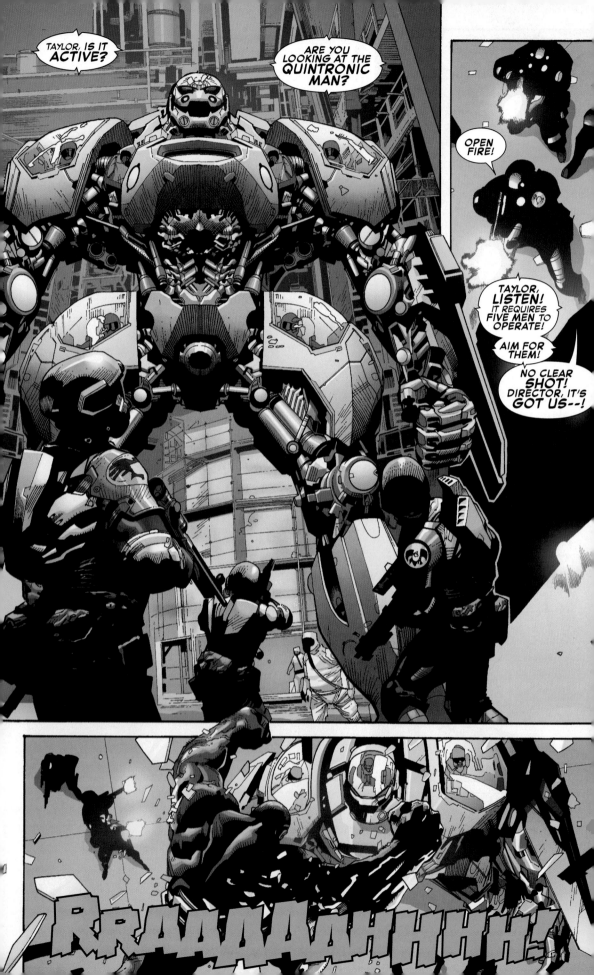

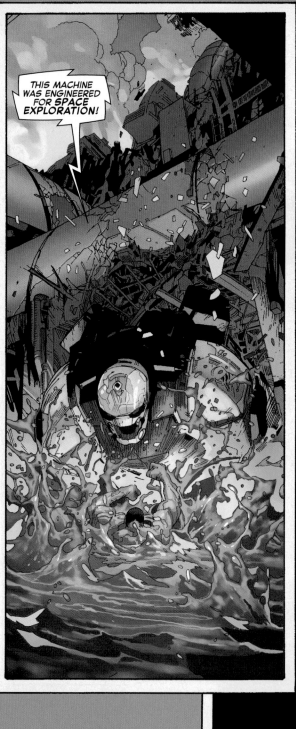

THIS MACHINE WAS ENGINEERED FOR SPACE EXPLORATION!

IT CAN WITHSTAND ANY TEMPERATURE!

ANY PRESSURE!

CAN YOU?

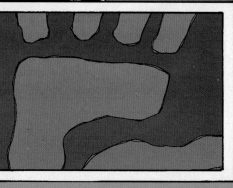

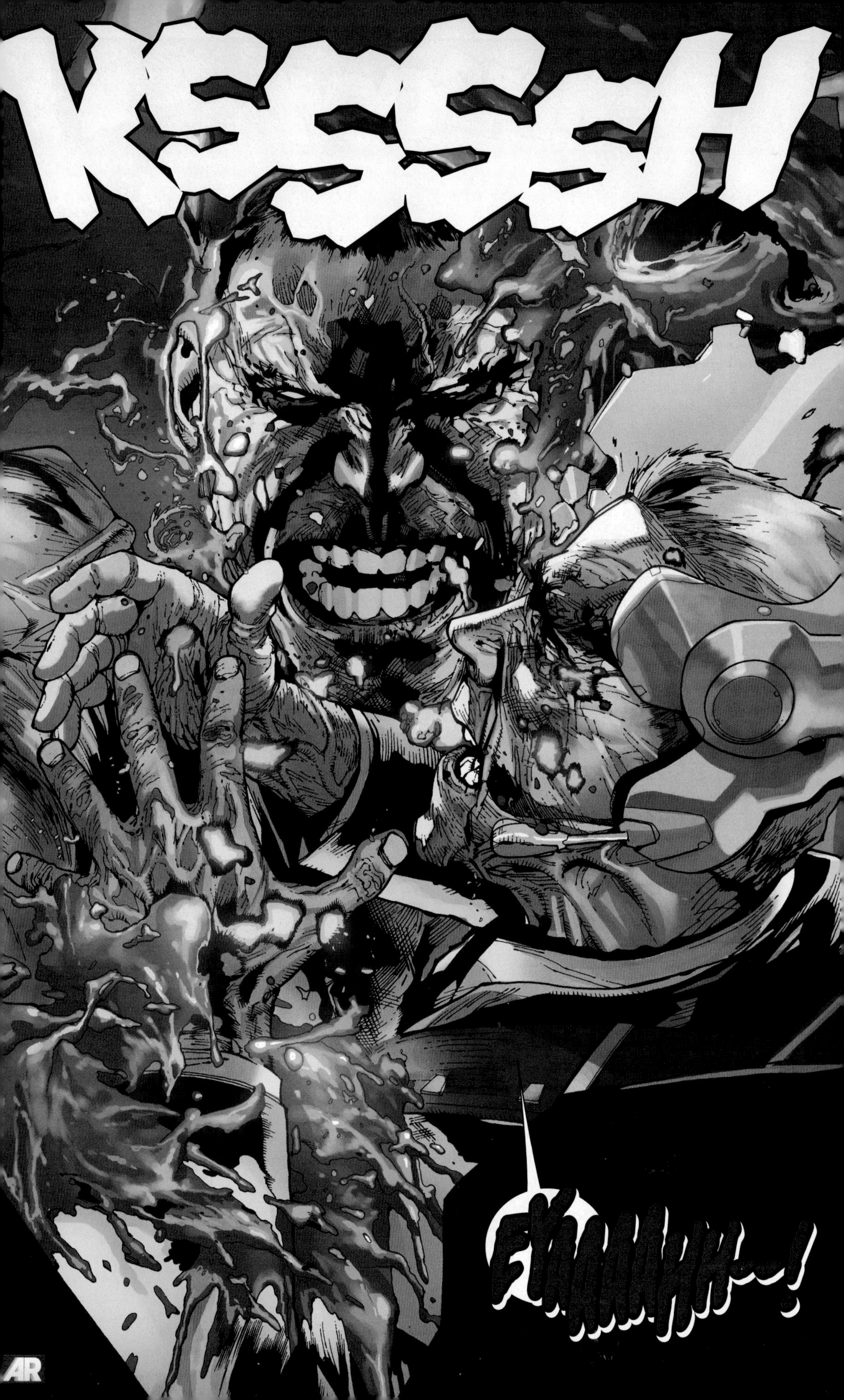
KSSSSH
EYAAAAHH...!

WHABOOM

... WOW!

TAYLOR, I DIDN'T *GET* THAT! COME *AGAIN?*

UMM... WE'RE...

...WE'RE *GOOD* HERE, DIRECTOR! AS FAR AS *HULK* GOES, WE'LL ENACT THE STANDARD *EXTRACTION PROCEDURE--*

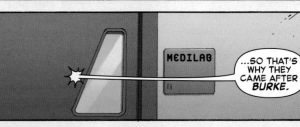

"--AS SOON AS HE'S COOL TO THE *TOUCH!*"

MEDILAB

...SO THAT'S WHY THEY CAME AFTER *BURKE.*

TWENTY-FOUR HOURS LATER.

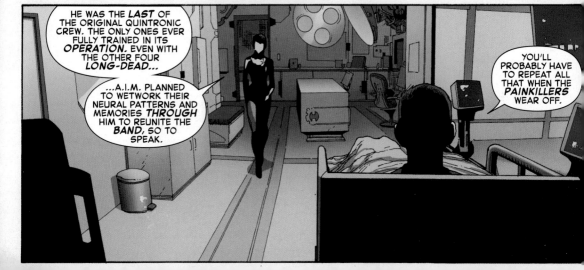

HE WAS THE *LAST* OF THE ORIGINAL QUINTRONIC CREW. THE ONLY ONES EVER FULLY TRAINED IN ITS *OPERATION.* EVEN WITH THE OTHER FOUR *LONG-DEAD...*

...A.I.M. PLANNED TO WETWORK THEIR NEURAL PATTERNS AND MEMORIES *THROUGH* HIM TO REUNITE THE *BAND,* SO TO SPEAK.

YOU'LL PROBABLY HAVE TO REPEAT ALL THAT WHEN THE *PAINKILLERS* WEAR OFF.

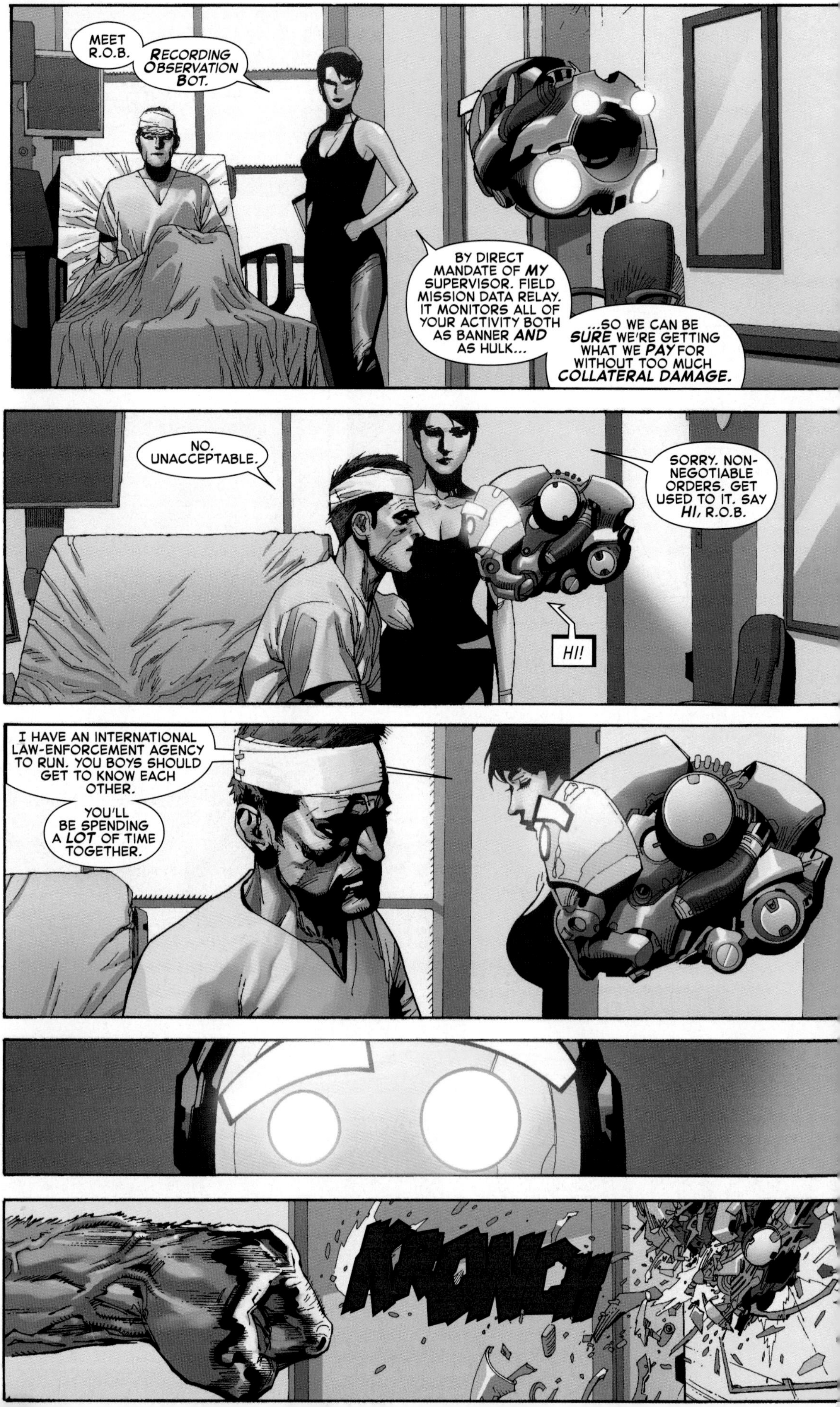
MEET R.O.B.
RECORDING OBSERVATION BOT.
BY DIRECT MANDATE OF MY SUPERVISOR. FIELD MISSION DATA RELAY. IT MONITORS ALL OF YOUR ACTIVITY BOTH AS BANNER AND AS HULK...
...SO WE CAN BE SURE WE'RE GETTING WHAT WE PAY FOR WITHOUT TOO MUCH COLLATERAL DAMAGE.
NO. UNACCEPTABLE.
SORRY. NON-NEGOTIABLE ORDERS. GET USED TO IT. SAY HI, R.O.B.
HI!
I HAVE AN INTERNATIONAL LAW-ENFORCEMENT AGENCY TO RUN. YOU BOYS SHOULD GET TO KNOW EACH OTHER.
YOU'LL BE SPENDING A LOT OF TIME TOGETHER.

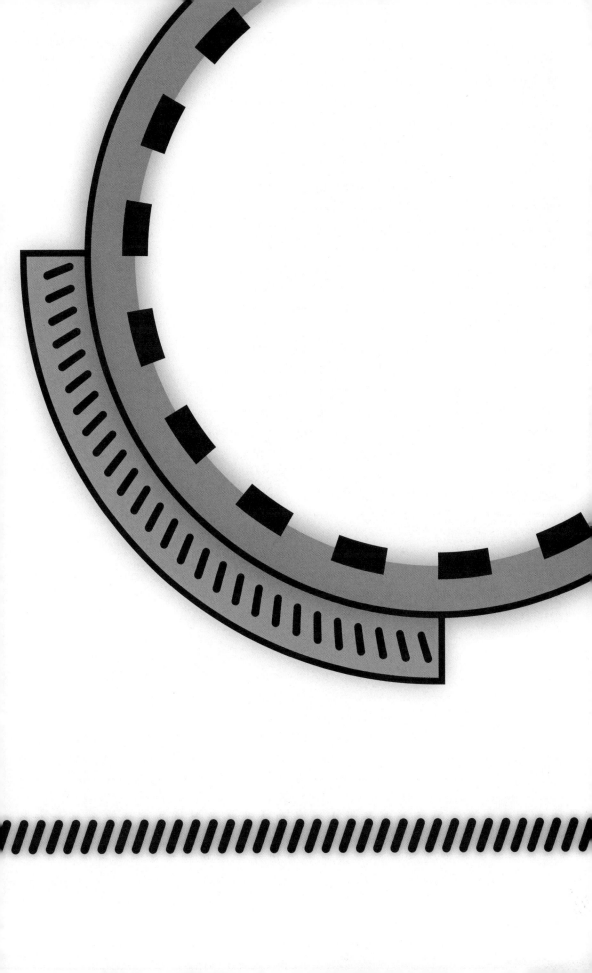

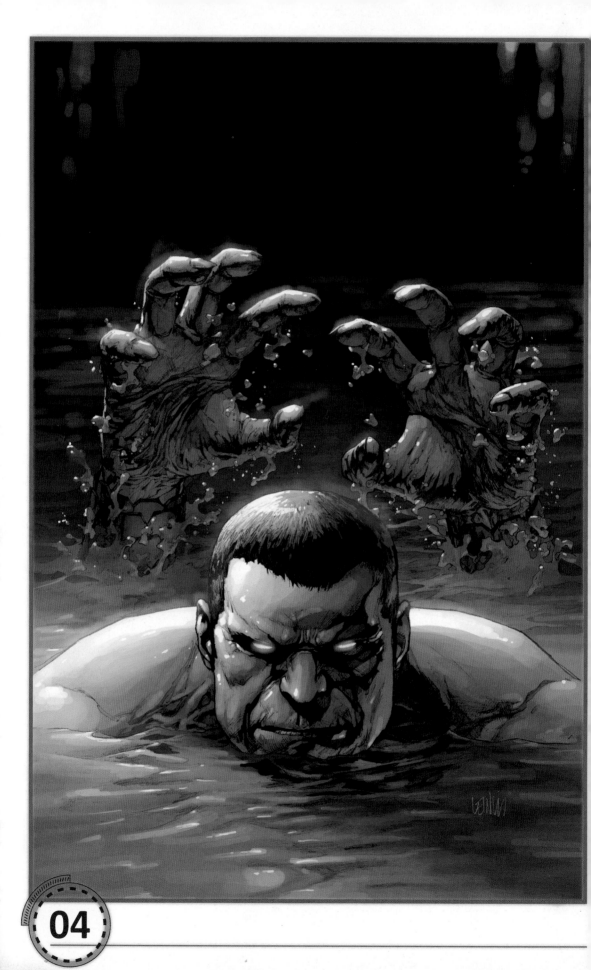

04

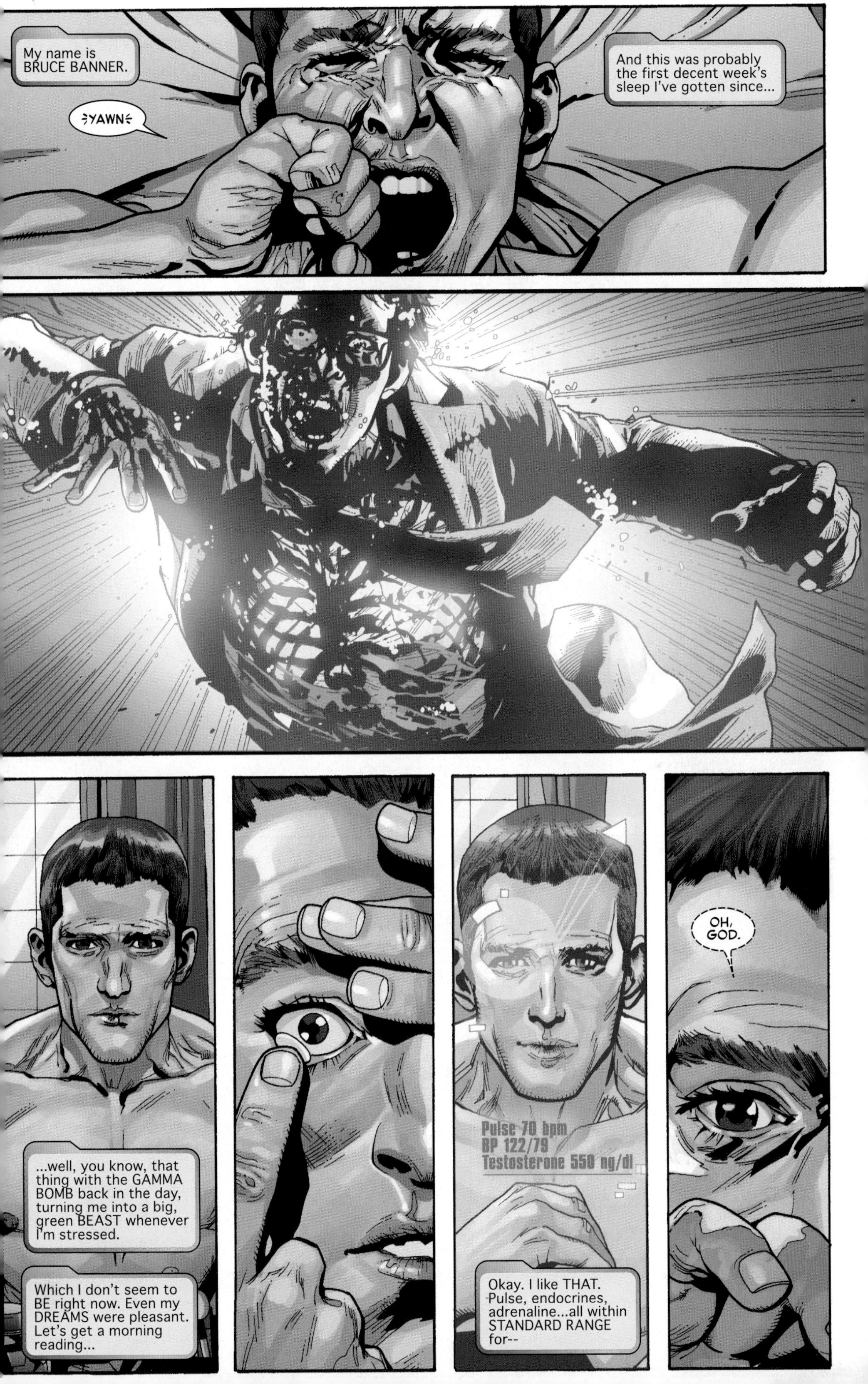

My name is BRUCE BANNER.
≑YAWN≑
And this was probably the first decent week's sleep I've gotten since...
...well, you know, that thing with the GAMMA BOMB back in the day, turning me into a big, green BEAST whenever I'm stressed.
Which I don't seem to BE right now. Even my DREAMS were pleasant. Let's get a morning reading...
Pulse 70 bpm
BP 122/79
Testosterone 550 ng/dl
Okay. I like THAT. Pulse, endocrines, adrenaline...all within STANDARD RANGE for--
OH, GOD.

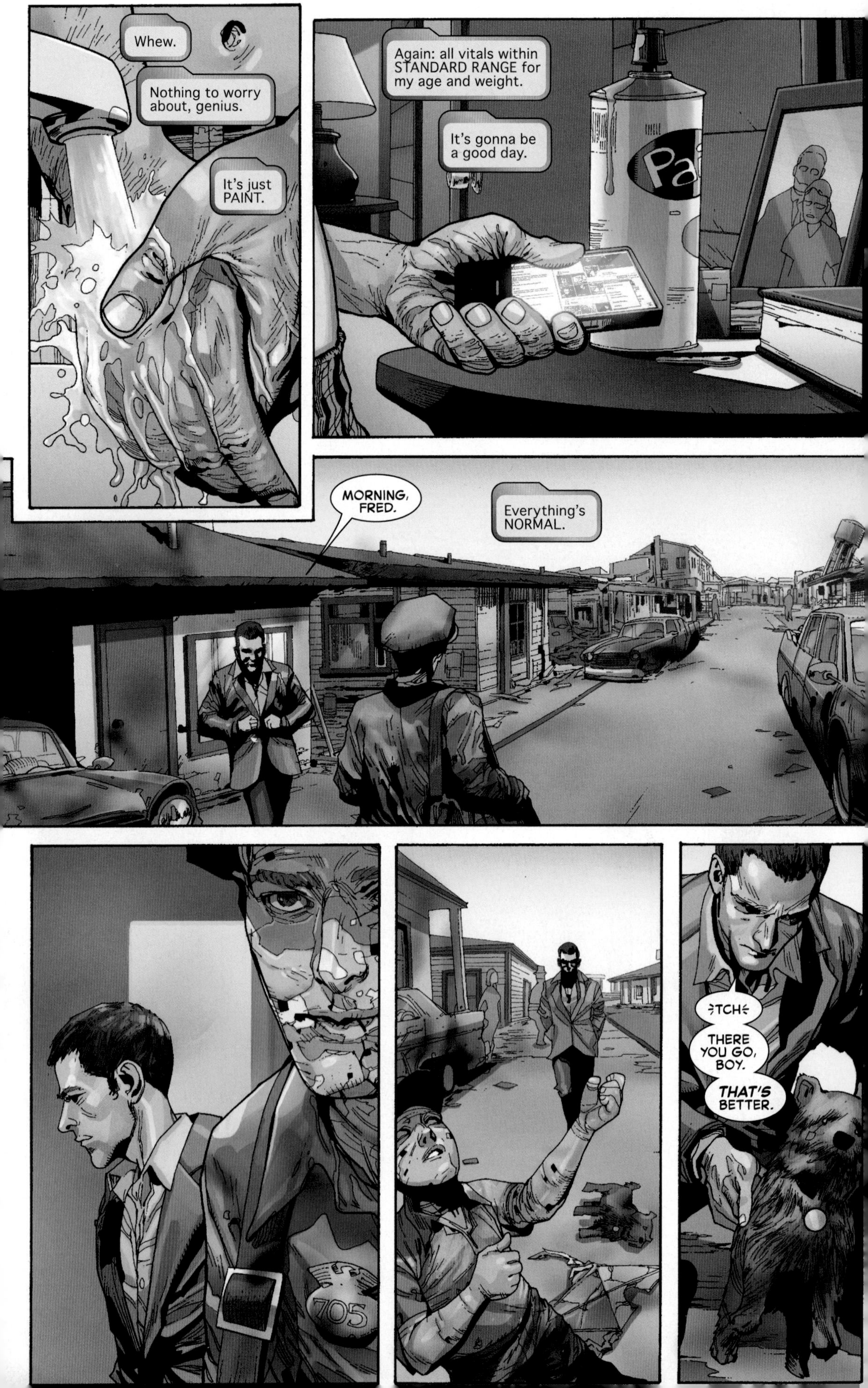

Whew.
Nothing to worry about, genius.
It's just PAINT.
Again: all vitals within STANDARD RANGE for my age and weight.
It's gonna be a good day.
MORNING, FRED.
Everything's NORMAL.
705
TCH
THERE YOU GO, BOY.
THAT'S BETTER.

Monday morning. Time to introduce myself to my new ASSISTANTS.

GOOD MORNING, DOCTORS. A PLEASURE. I AM DR. BRUCE BANNER, 21-TIME NOBEL PRIZE LOSER.

AND YOUR TASK IS TO HELP ME BREAK THAT STREAK.

I'M SURE YOU HAVE QUESTIONS?

Patricia Wolman, Climatologist AND Astrophysicist.

Melinda Leucenstern, Microneural Biologist.

Randy Jessup, Renewable Energies Specialist.

Daman Veteri, Molecular Engineer.

DOCTOR, CAN WE PLEAS--

I EXPECTED MORE--

I'LL START. DOC, ARE--

CAN WE DISCUSS--

LET ME ANSWER THE ONE YOU'RE ALL TOO POLITE TO LEAD WITH. THE REASON OUR STAFF IS SMALL IS BECAUSE--

WHAT DO YOU MEAN THERE'S NO INTERNET CONNECTION? DAMN IT!

TAP TAP TAP

AR

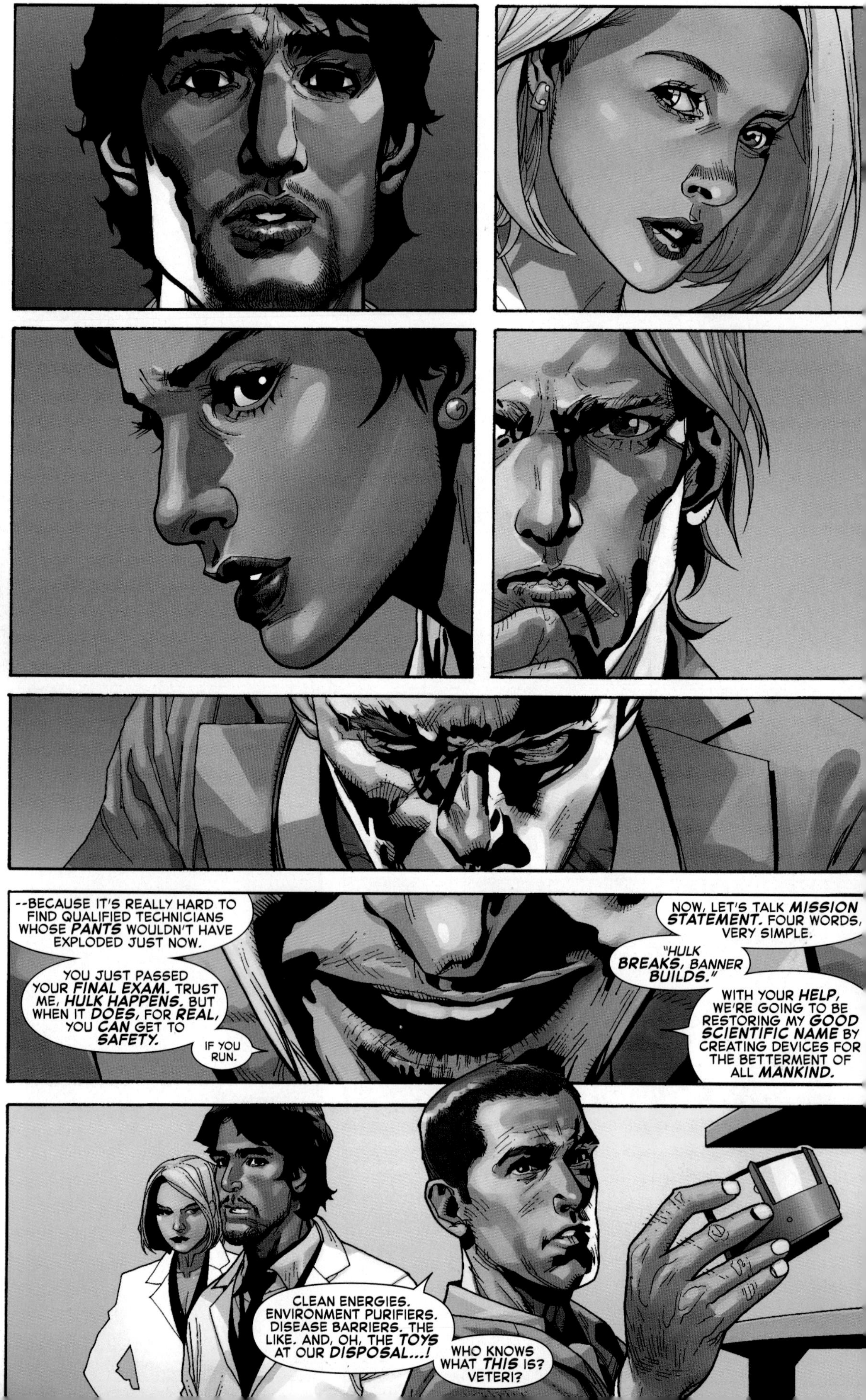
--BECAUSE IT'S REALLY HARD TO FIND QUALIFIED TECHNICIANS WHOSE PANTS WOULDN'T HAVE EXPLODED JUST NOW.
YOU JUST PASSED YOUR FINAL EXAM. TRUST ME, HULK HAPPENS. BUT WHEN IT DOES, FOR REAL, YOU CAN GET TO SAFETY.
IF YOU RUN.
NOW, LET'S TALK MISSION STATEMENT. FOUR WORDS, VERY SIMPLE.
"HULK BREAKS, BANNER BUILDS."
WITH YOUR HELP, WE'RE GOING TO BE RESTORING MY GOOD SCIENTIFIC NAME BY CREATING DEVICES FOR THE BETTERMENT OF ALL MANKIND.
CLEAN ENERGIES. ENVIRONMENT PURIFIERS. DISEASE BARRIERS. THE LIKE. AND, OH, THE TOYS AT OUR DISPOSAL...!
WHO KNOWS WHAT THIS IS? VETERI?

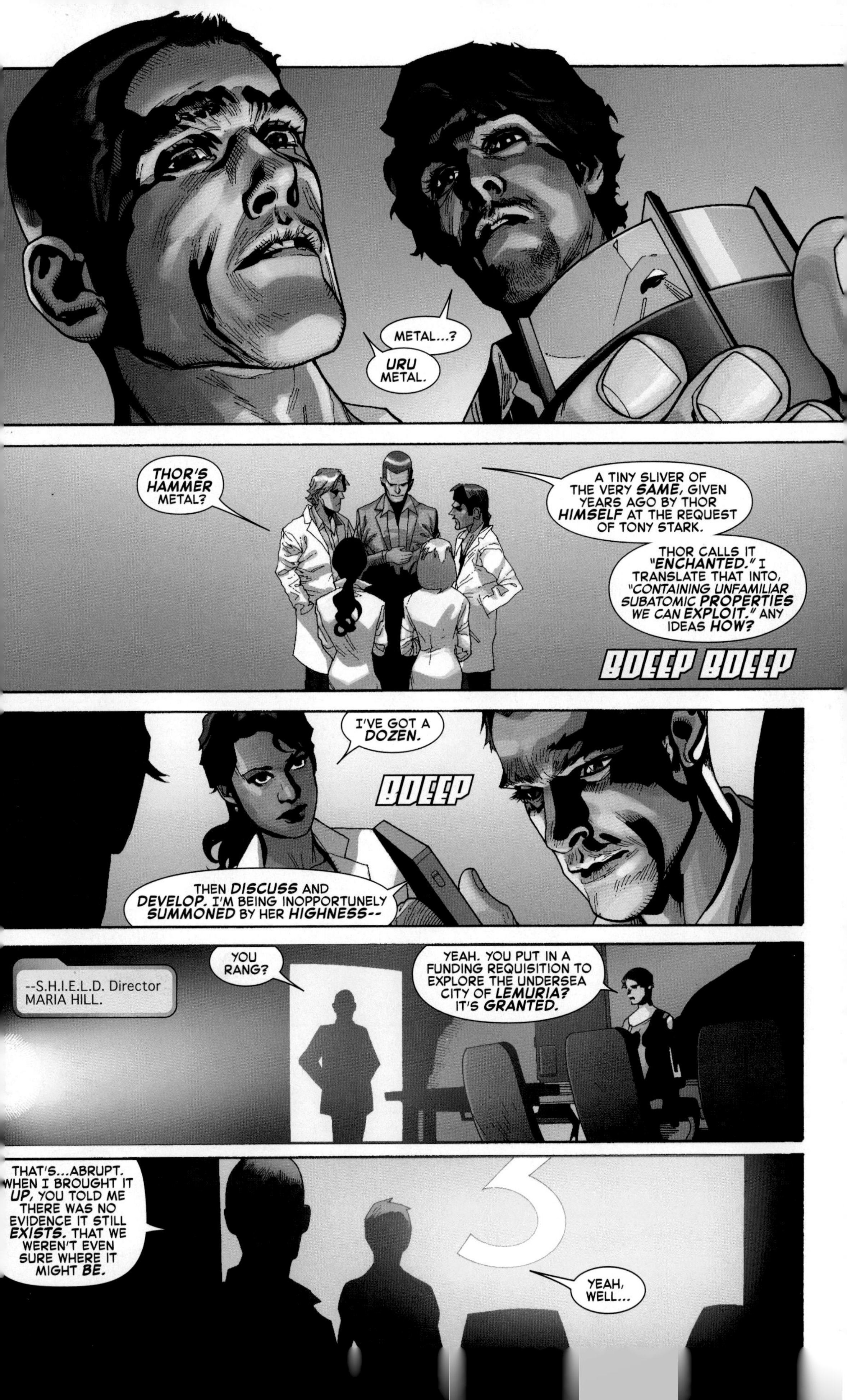
METAL...?
URU METAL.
THOR'S HAMMER METAL?
A TINY SLIVER OF THE VERY SAME, GIVEN YEARS AGO BY THOR HIMSELF AT THE REQUEST OF TONY STARK.
THOR CALLS IT "ENCHANTED." I TRANSLATE THAT INTO, "CONTAINING UNFAMILIAR SUBATOMIC PROPERTIES WE CAN EXPLOIT." ANY IDEAS HOW?
BDEEP BDEEP
I'VE GOT A DOZEN.
BDEEP
THEN DISCUSS AND DEVELOP. I'M BEING INOPPORTUNELY SUMMONED BY HER HIGHNESS--
--S.H.I.E.L.D. Director MARIA HILL.
YOU RANG?
YEAH. YOU PUT IN A FUNDING REQUISITION TO EXPLORE THE UNDERSEA CITY OF LEMURIA? IT'S GRANTED.
THAT'S...ABRUPT. WHEN I BROUGHT IT UP, YOU TOLD ME THERE WAS NO EVIDENCE IT STILL EXISTS. THAT WE WEREN'T EVEN SURE WHERE IT MIGHT BE.
YEAH, WELL...

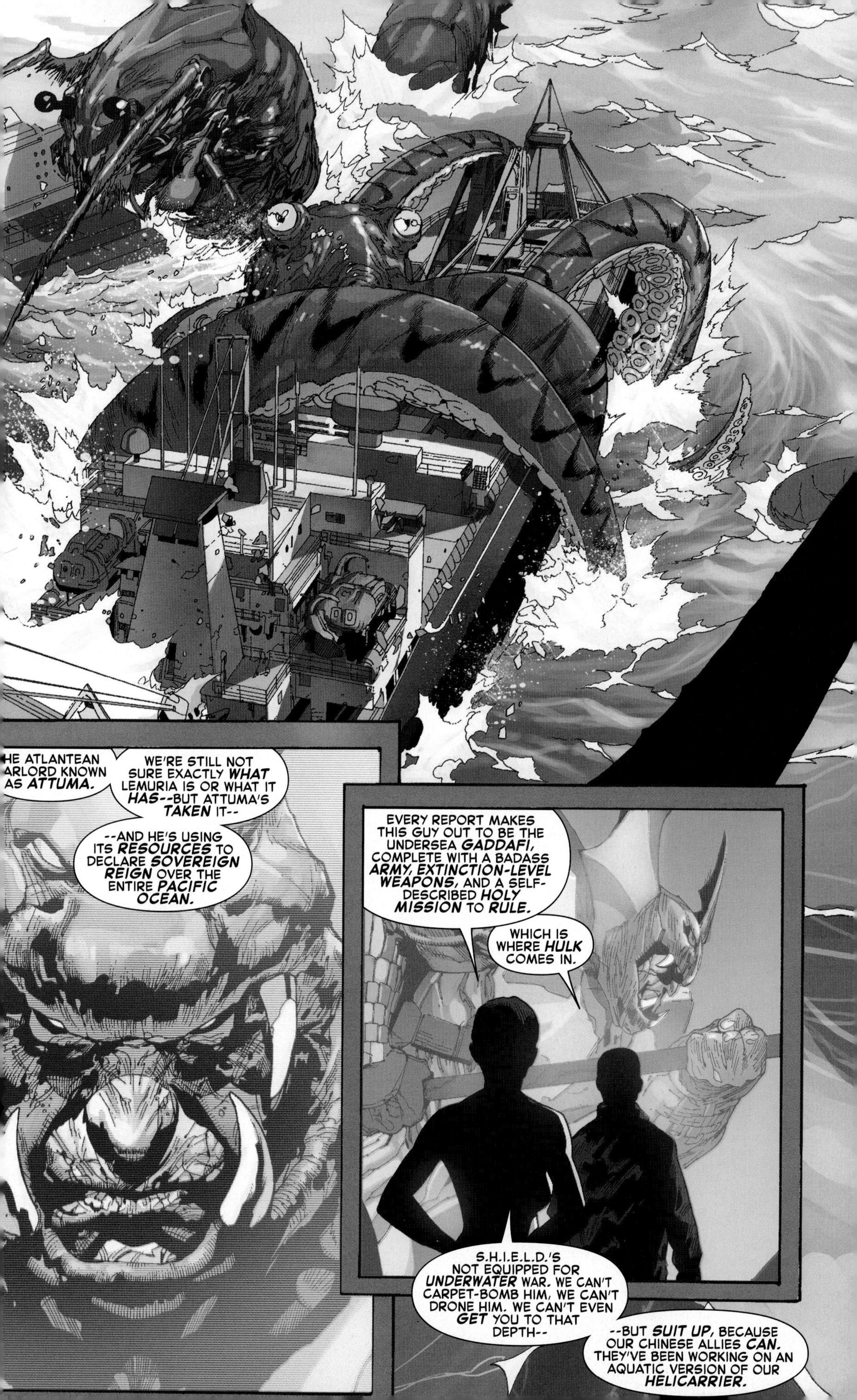

HE ATLANTEAN ARLORD KNOWN AS ATTUMA.
WE'RE STILL NOT SURE EXACTLY WHAT LEMURIA IS OR WHAT IT HAS--BUT ATTUMA'S TAKEN IT--
--AND HE'S USING ITS RESOURCES TO DECLARE SOVEREIGN REIGN OVER THE ENTIRE PACIFIC OCEAN.
EVERY REPORT MAKES THIS GUY OUT TO BE THE UNDERSEA GADDAFI, COMPLETE WITH A BADASS ARMY, EXTINCTION-LEVEL WEAPONS, AND A SELF-DESCRIBED HOLY MISSION TO RULE.
WHICH IS WHERE HULK COMES IN.
S.H.I.E.L.D.'S NOT EQUIPPED FOR UNDERWATER WAR. WE CAN'T CARPET-BOMB HIM, WE CAN'T DRONE HIM. WE CAN'T EVEN GET YOU TO THAT DEPTH--
--BUT SUIT UP, BECAUSE OUR CHINESE ALLIES CAN. THEY'VE BEEN WORKING ON AN AQUATIC VERSION OF OUR HELICARRIER.

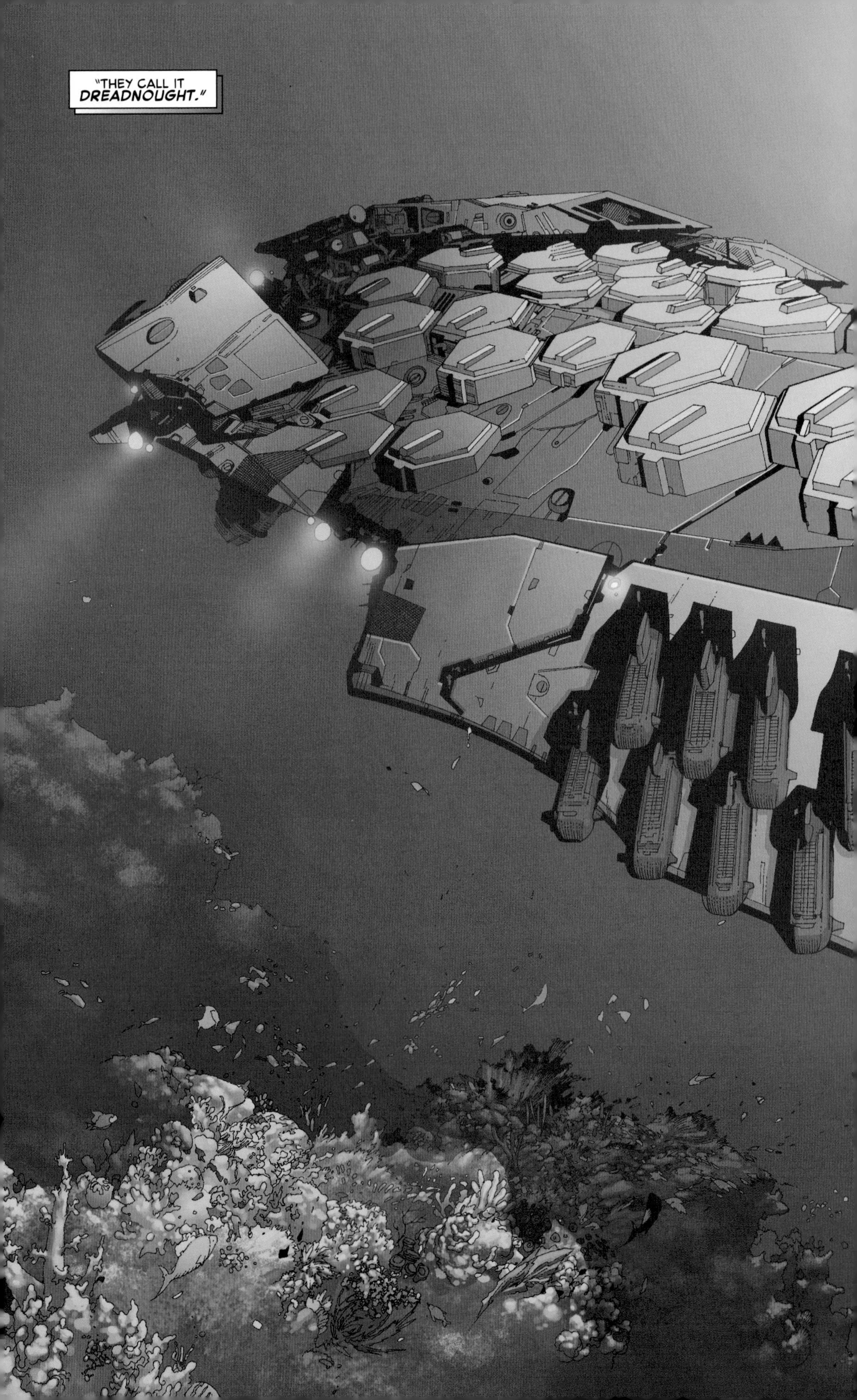
"THEY CALL IT DREADNOUGHT."

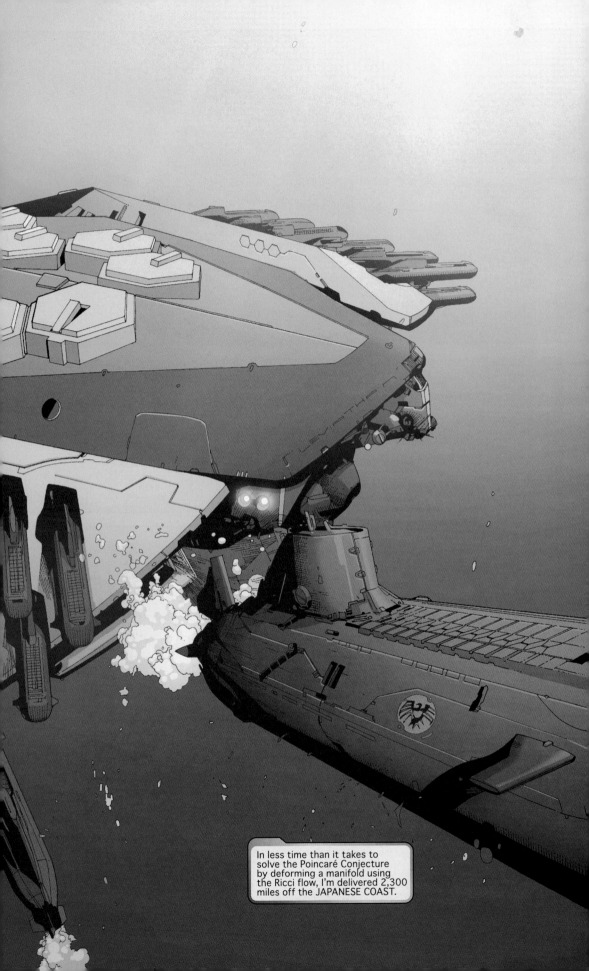

In less time than it takes to solve the Poincaré Conjecture by deforming a manifold using the Ricci flow, I'm delivered 2,300 miles off the JAPANESE COAST.

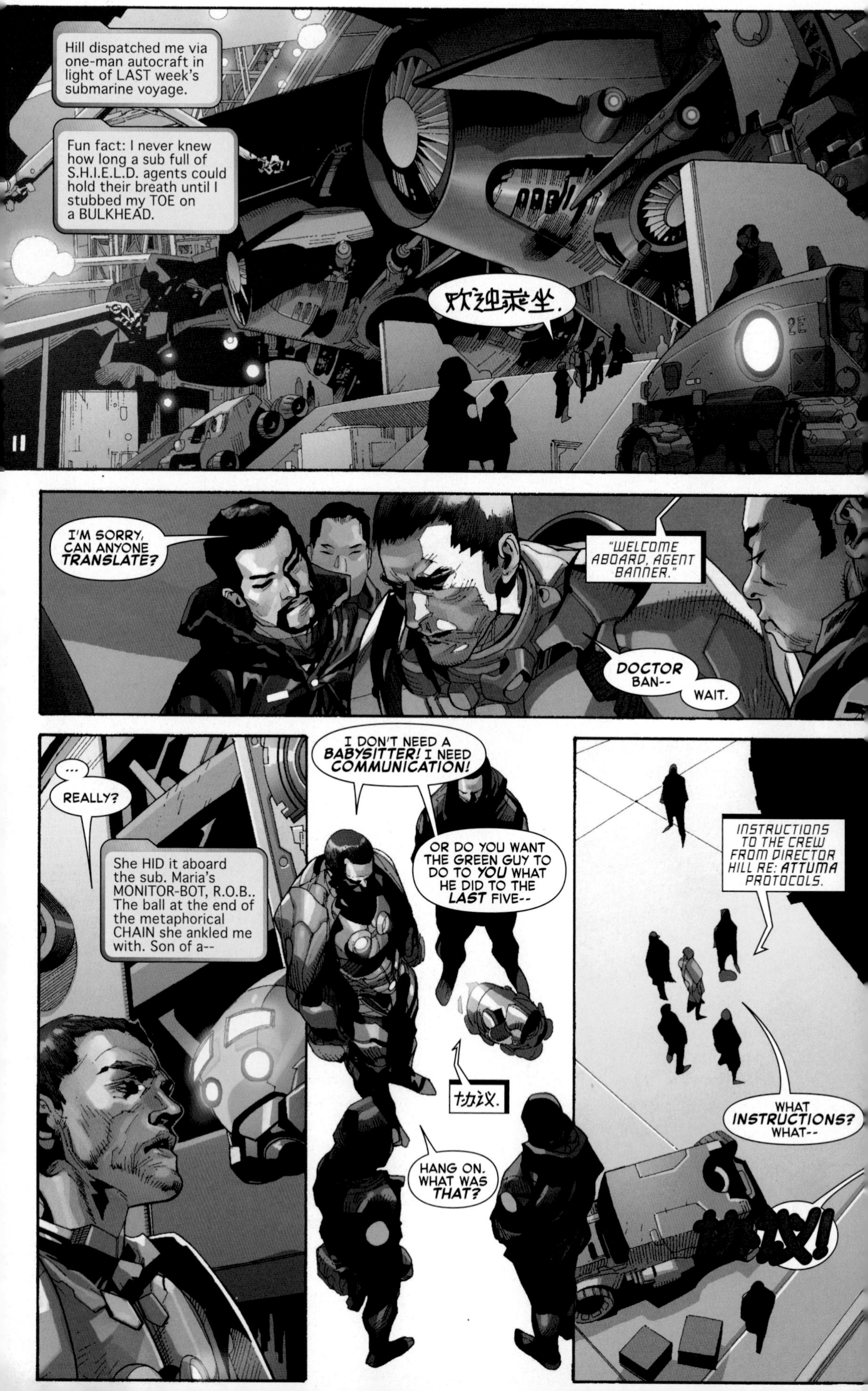
Hill dispatched me via one-man autocraft in light of LAST week's submarine voyage.
Fun fact: I never knew how long a sub full of S.H.I.E.L.D. agents could hold their breath until I stubbed my TOE on a BULKHEAD.
欢迎乘坐.
I'M SORRY, CAN ANYONE TRANSLATE?
"WELCOME ABOARD, AGENT BANNER."
DOCTOR BAN--
WAIT.
...
REALLY?
She HID it aboard the sub. Maria's MONITOR-BOT, R.O.B.. The ball at the end of the metaphorical CHAIN she ankled me with. Son of a--
I DON'T NEED A BABYSITTER! I NEED COMMUNICATION!
OR DO YOU WANT THE GREEN GUY TO DO TO YOU WHAT HE DID TO THE LAST FIVE--
协议.
HANG ON. WHAT WAS THAT?
INSTRUCTIONS TO THE CREW FROM DIRECTOR HILL RE: ATTUMA PROTOCOLS.
WHAT INSTRUCTIONS? WHAT--

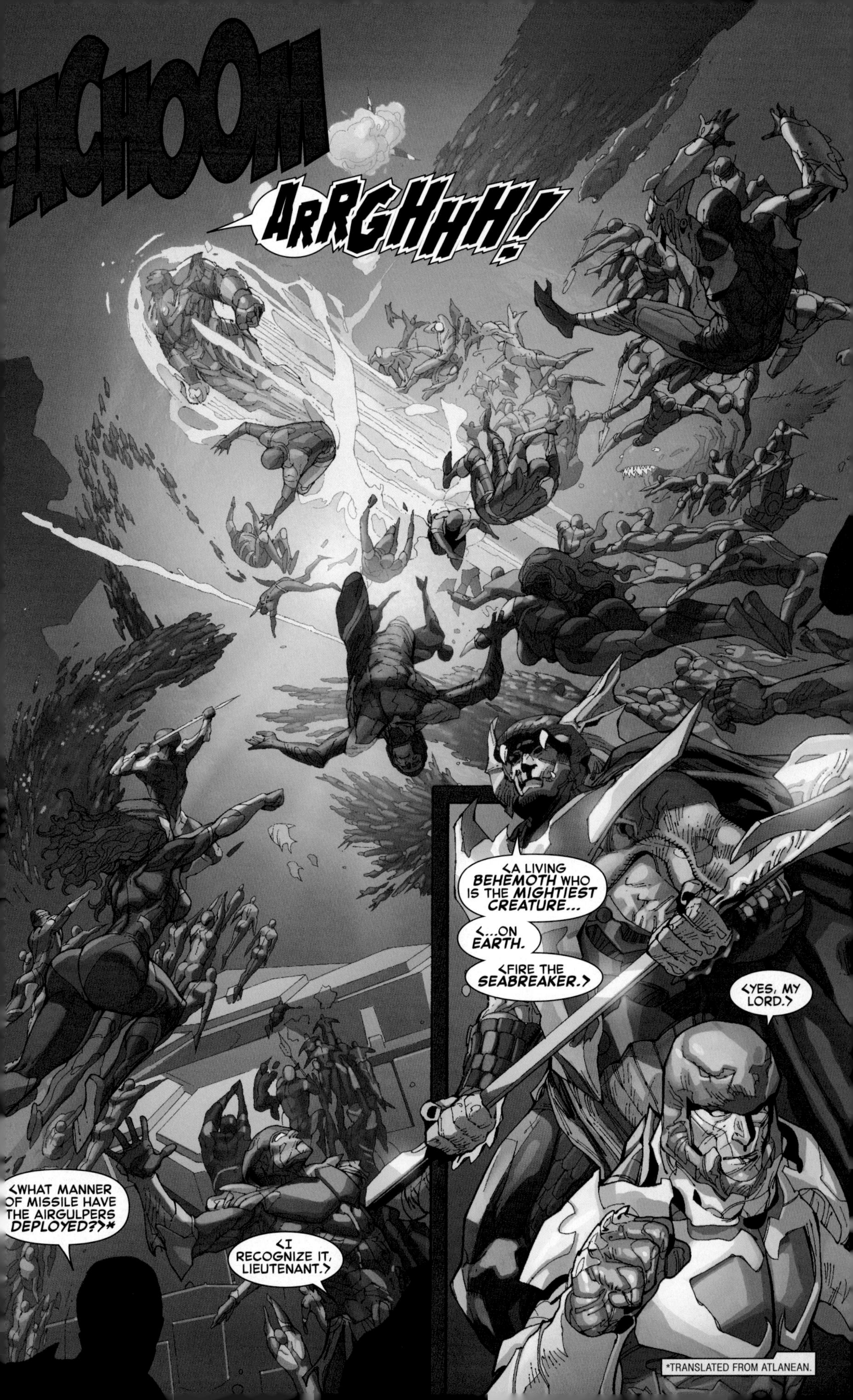
ACHOOM
ARRGHHH!
<A LIVING BEHEMOTH WHO IS THE MIGHTIEST CREATURE...
<...ON EARTH.
<FIRE THE SEABREAKER.>
<YES, MY LORD.>
<WHAT MANNER OF MISSILE HAVE THE AIRGULPERS DEPLOYED?>*
<I RECOGNIZE IT, LIEUTENANT.>
*TRANSLATED FROM ATLANEAN.

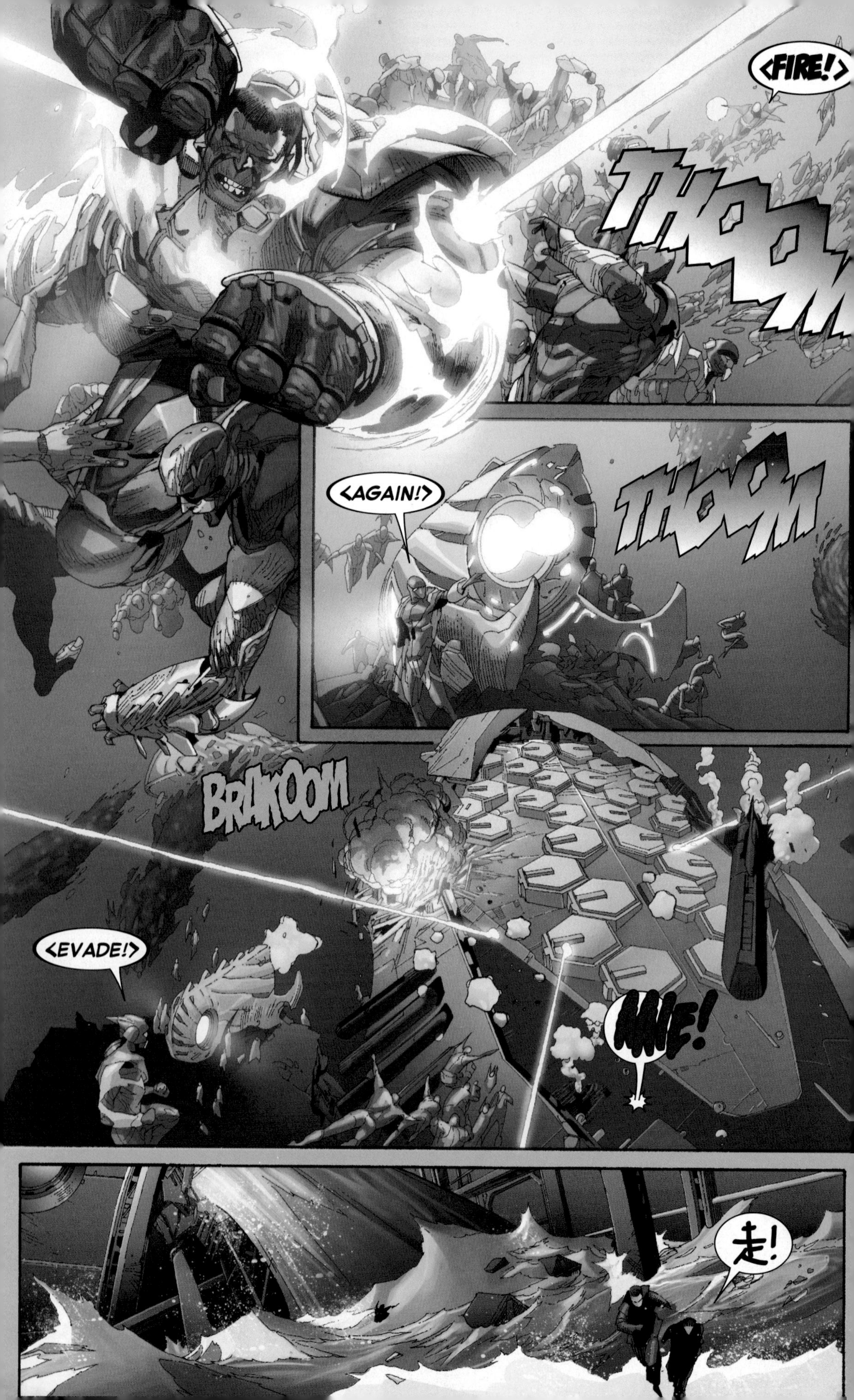
<FIRE!>
THOOM
<AGAIN!>
THOOM
BRAKOOM
<EVADE!>
MIE!
走!

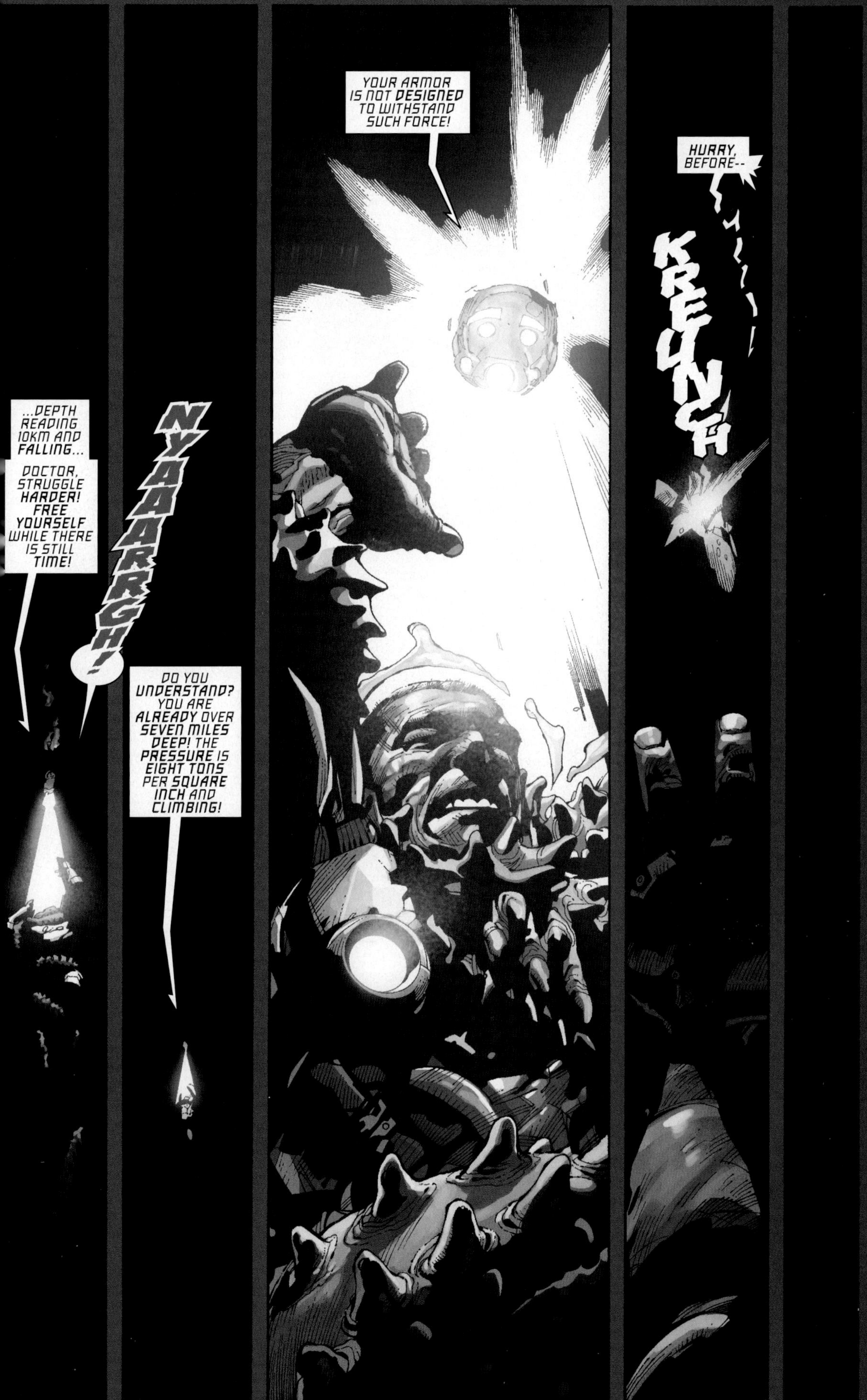
...DEPTH READING 10KM AND FALLING...
DOCTOR, STRUGGLE HARDER! FREE YOURSELF WHILE THERE IS STILL TIME!
NYAAARRGH!
DO YOU UNDERSTAND? YOU ARE ALREADY OVER SEVEN MILES DEEP! THE PRESSURE IS EIGHT TONS PER SQUARE INCH AND CLIMBING!
YOUR ARMOR IS NOT DESIGNED TO WITHSTAND SUCH FORCE!
HURRY, BEFORE--
KREUNCH

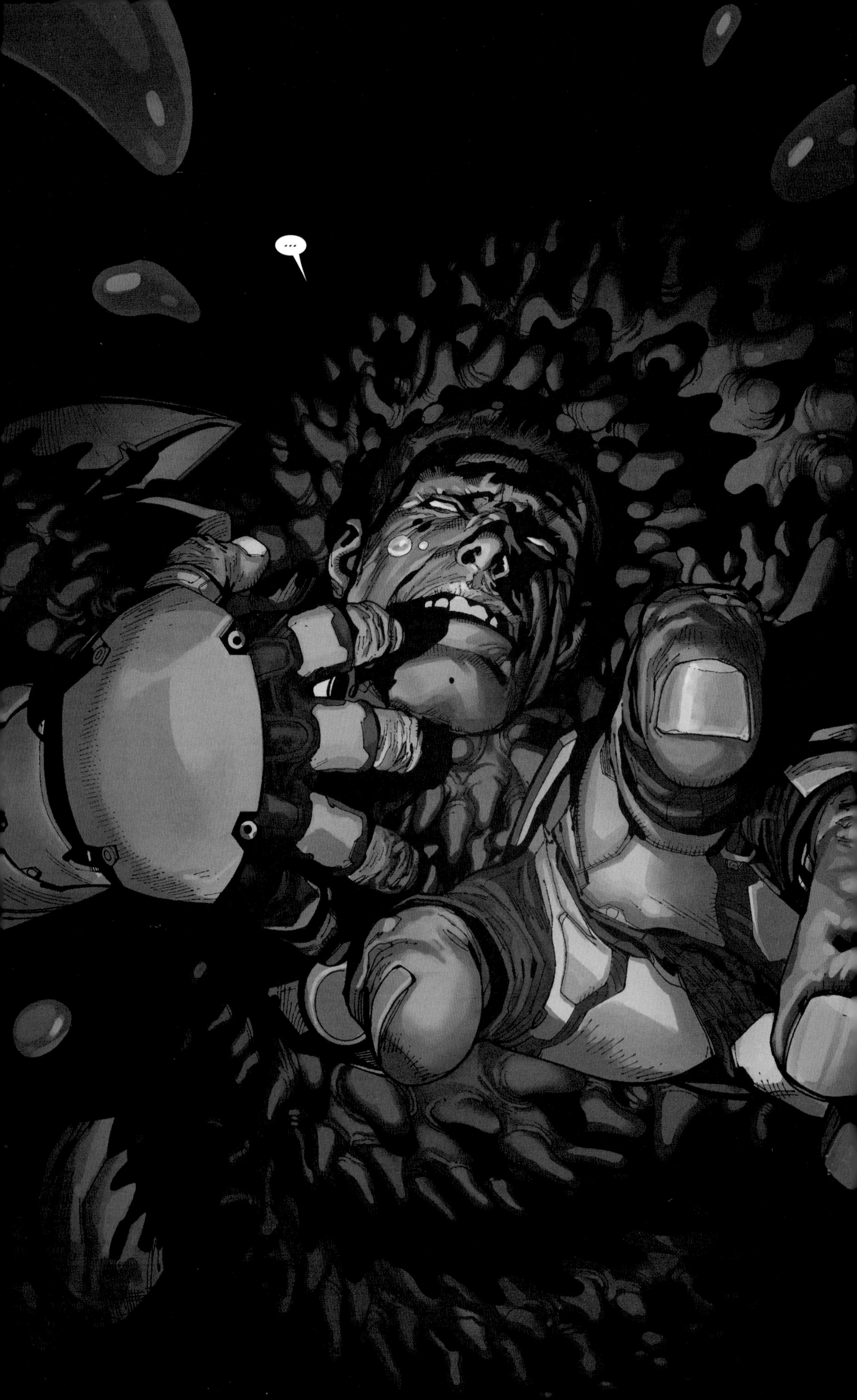
...

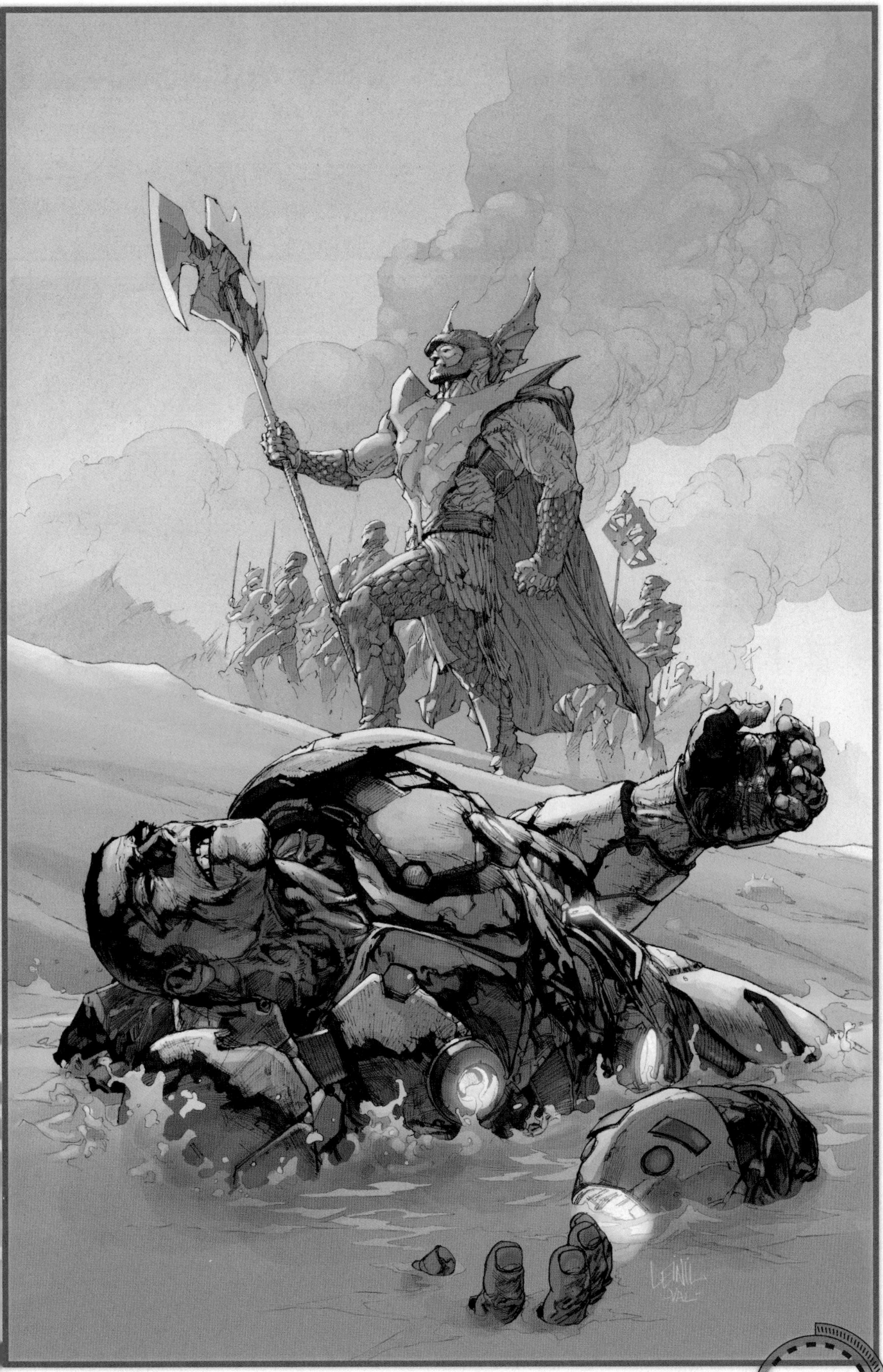

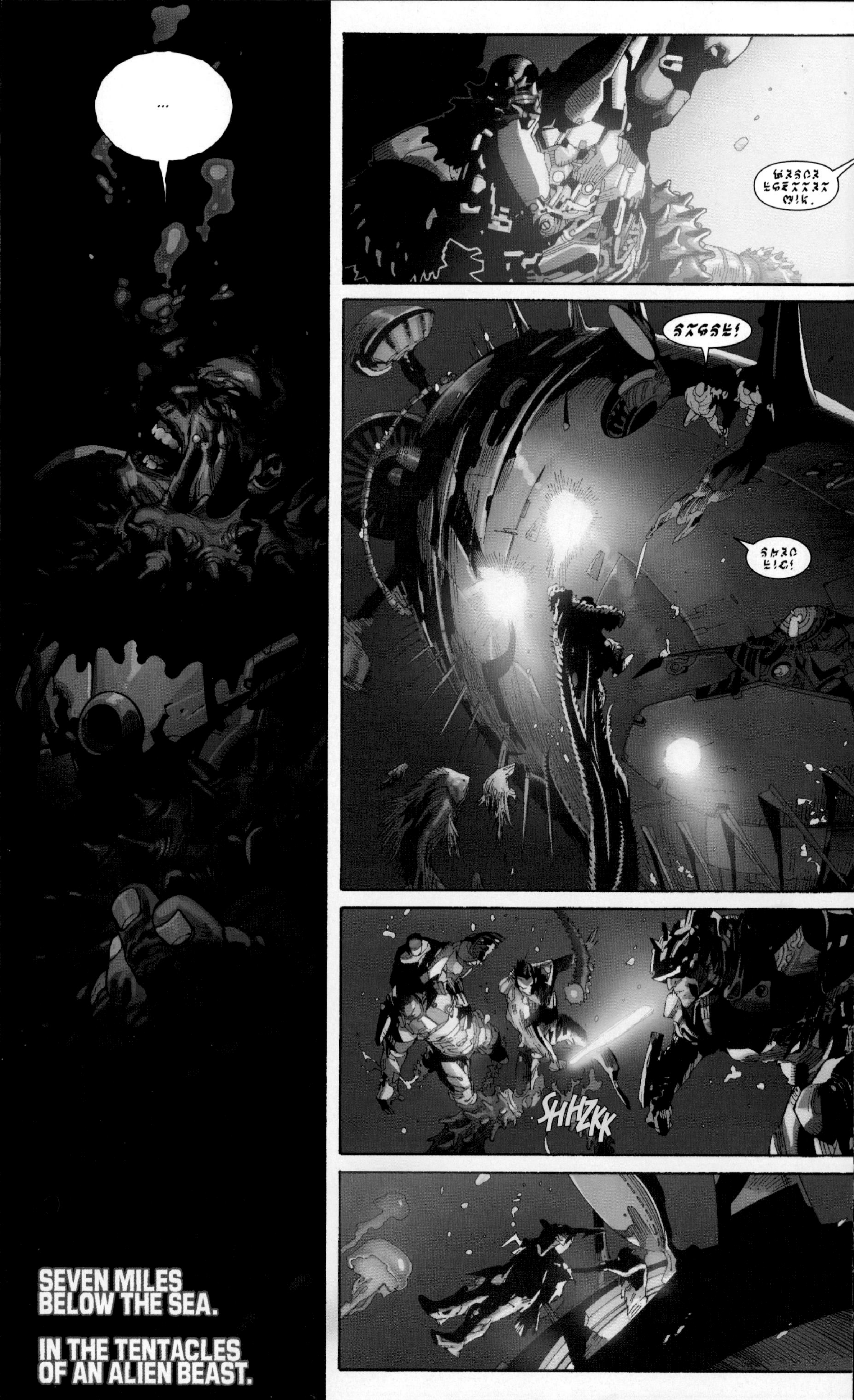
...
SHHZKK
SEVEN MILES BELOW THE SEA.
IN THE TENTACLES OF AN ALIEN BEAST.

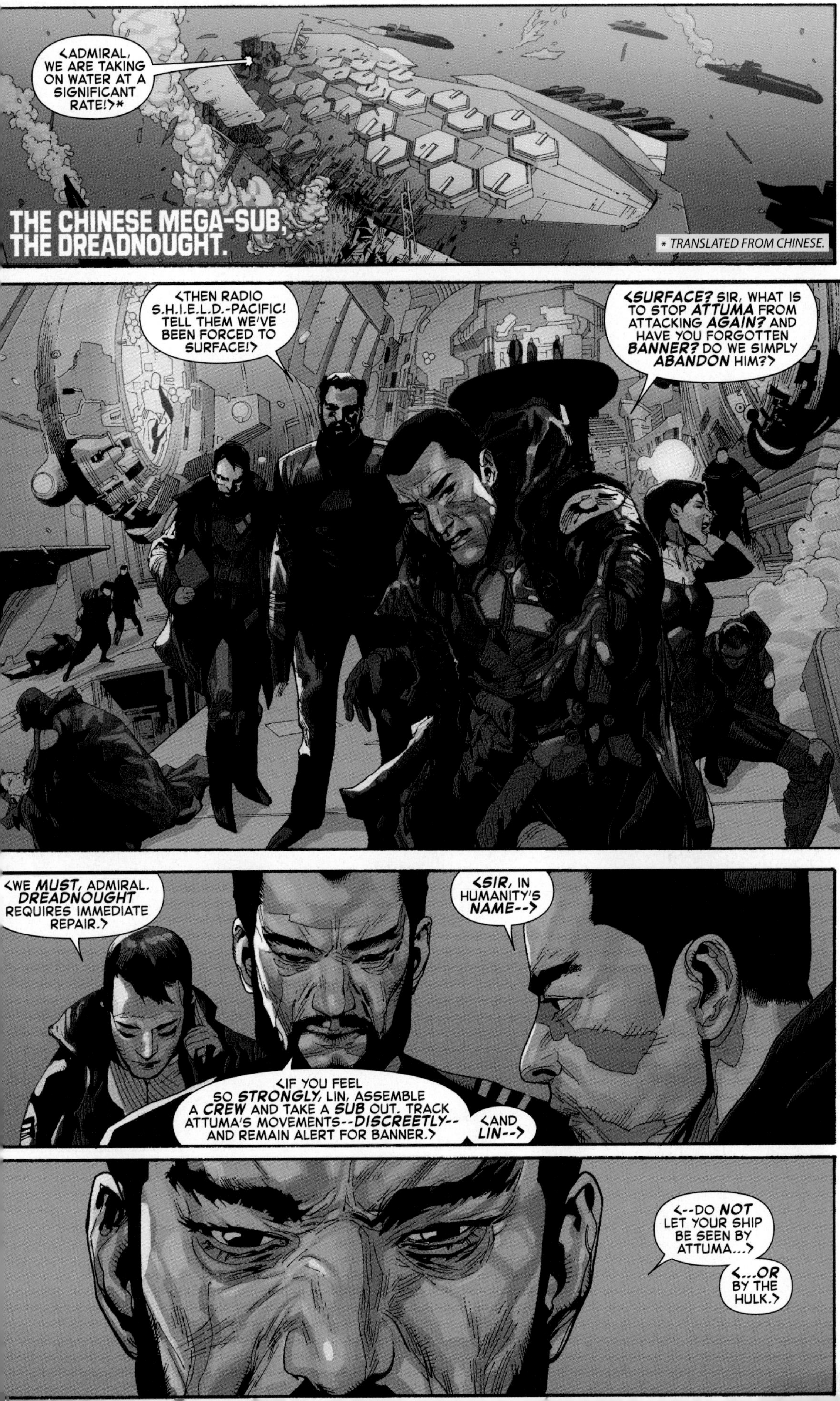
<ADMIRAL, WE ARE TAKING ON WATER AT A SIGNIFICANT RATE!>*
THE CHINESE MEGA-SUB, THE DREADNOUGHT.
* TRANSLATED FROM CHINESE.
<THEN RADIO S.H.I.E.L.D.-PACIFIC! TELL THEM WE'VE BEEN FORCED TO SURFACE!>
<SURFACE? SIR, WHAT IS TO STOP ATTUMA FROM ATTACKING AGAIN? AND HAVE YOU FORGOTTEN BANNER? DO WE SIMPLY ABANDON HIM?>
<WE MUST, ADMIRAL. DREADNOUGHT REQUIRES IMMEDIATE REPAIR.>
<SIR, IN HUMANITY'S NAME-->
<IF YOU FEEL SO STRONGLY, LIN, ASSEMBLE A CREW AND TAKE A SUB OUT. TRACK ATTUMA'S MOVEMENTS--DISCREETLY--AND REMAIN ALERT FOR BANNER.>
<AND LIN-->
<--DO NOT LET YOUR SHIP BE SEEN BY ATTUMA...>
<...OR BY THE HULK.>

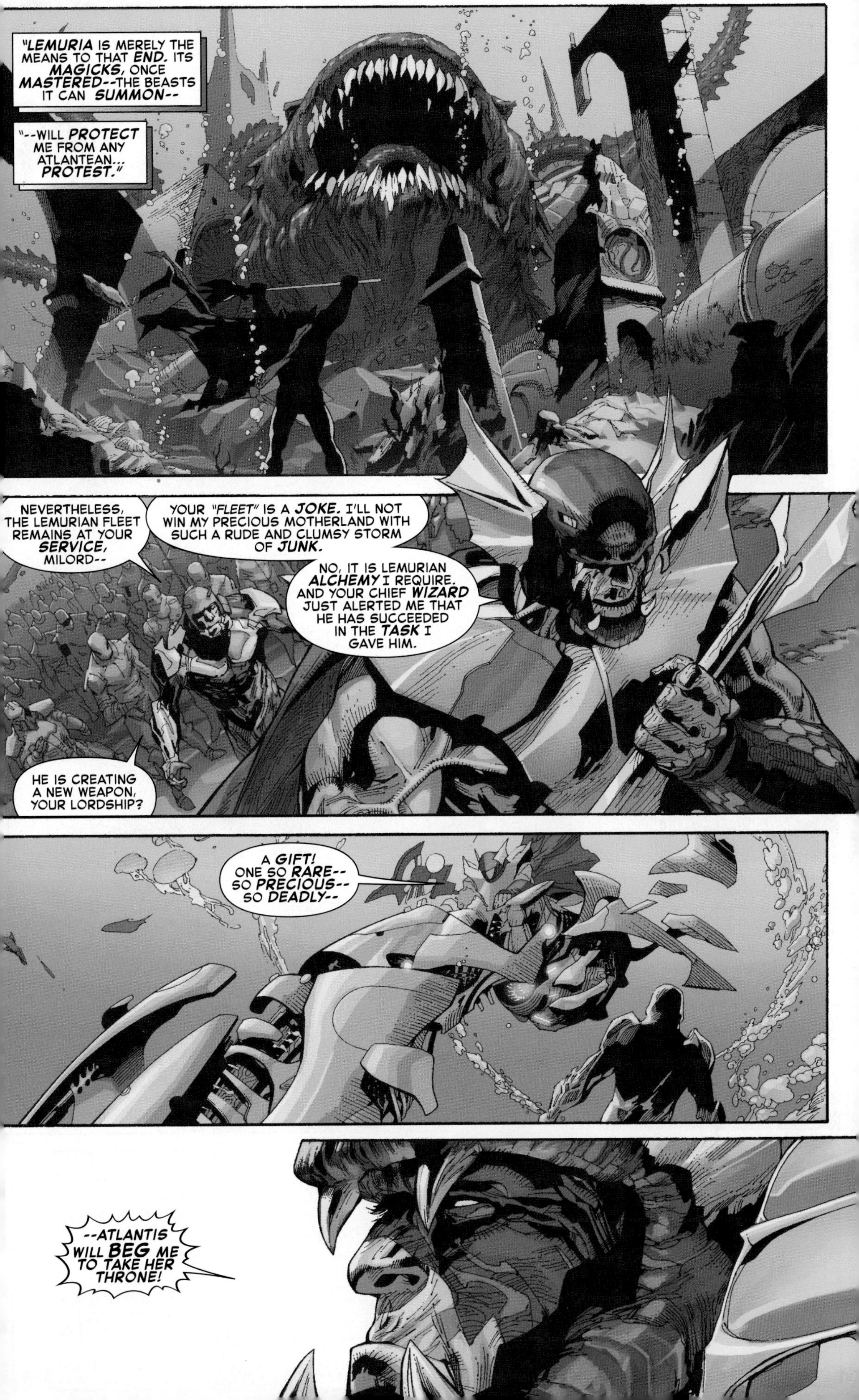
"LEMURIA IS MERELY THE MEANS TO THAT END. ITS MAGICKS, ONCE MASTERED--THE BEASTS IT CAN SUMMON--
"--WILL PROTECT ME FROM ANY ATLANTEAN... PROTEST."
NEVERTHELESS, THE LEMURIAN FLEET REMAINS AT YOUR SERVICE, MILORD--
YOUR "FLEET" IS A JOKE. I'LL NOT WIN MY PRECIOUS MOTHERLAND WITH SUCH A RUDE AND CLUMSY STORM OF JUNK.
NO, IT IS LEMURIAN ALCHEMY I REQUIRE. AND YOUR CHIEF WIZARD JUST ALERTED ME THAT HE HAS SUCCEEDED IN THE TASK I GAVE HIM.
HE IS CREATING A NEW WEAPON, YOUR LORDSHIP?
A GIFT! ONE SO RARE-- SO PRECIOUS-- SO DEADLY--
--ATLANTIS WILL BEG ME TO TAKE HER THRONE!

ʒUNNHʒ

Terrific. I'm a P.O.W. Thanks, Hulk.

DO NOT BE *AFRAID*, PINKLING. NO ONE WILL HARM YOU.

I'M... I'M NOT *DEAD*..?

⸻ TRANSLATION POD.

Oxygenation unit in the armor's still functioning...barely. I feel ASTHMATIC.

WE *RESCUED* YOU. THE *OTHER* YOU. BROUGHT YOU ABOARD THE *OPHION* TO SAFETY. I AM MARA.

AND I'M *BANNER*. I'M--

CHANGE FOR ME! BE THE *GREEN MAN!* BRING HIM *BACK!*

HA! DID I SPEAK WORDS OF AMUSEMENT?

KIND OF. I DON'T GET TOO MANY *REQUESTS* FOR "THE GREEN MAN."

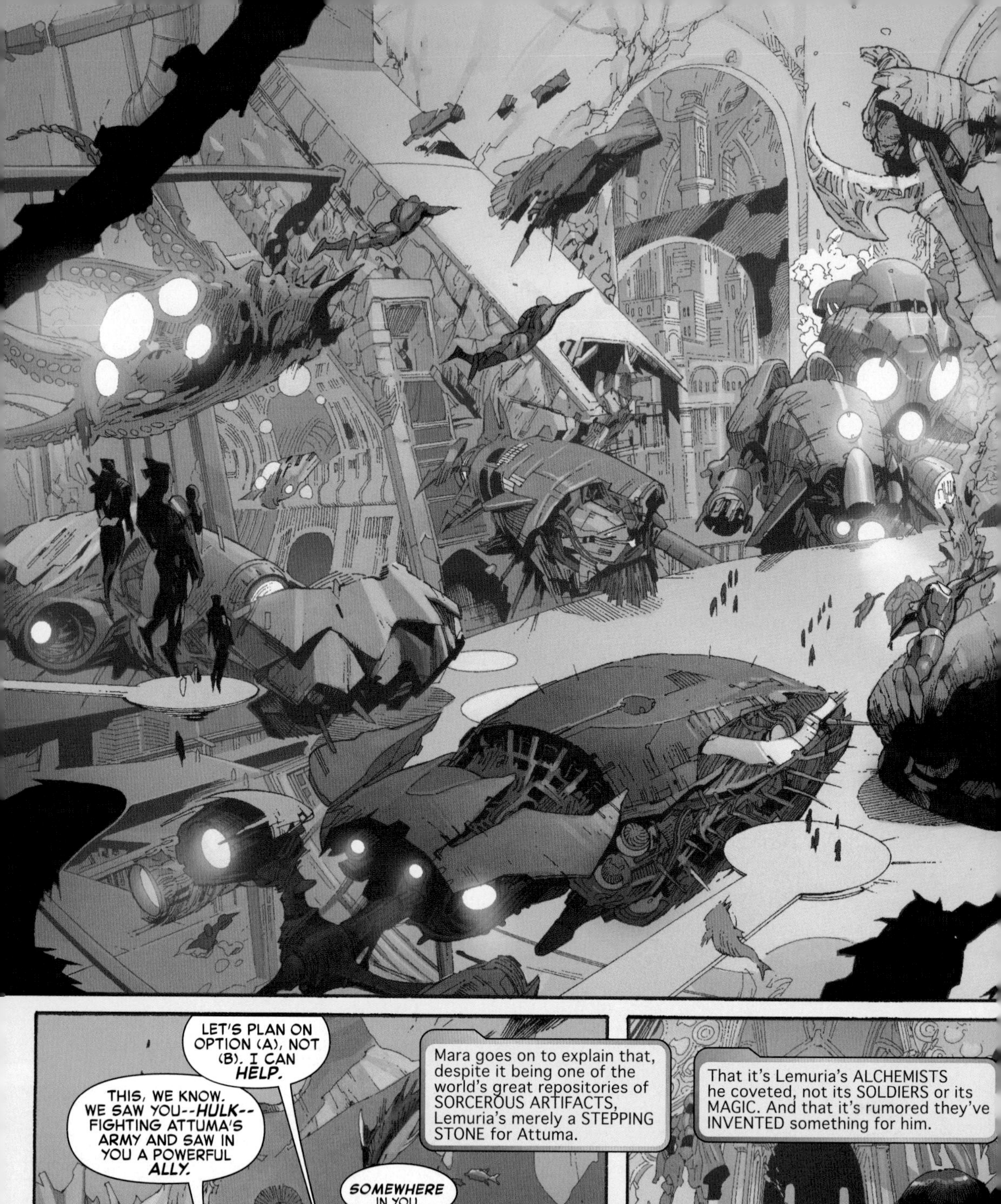

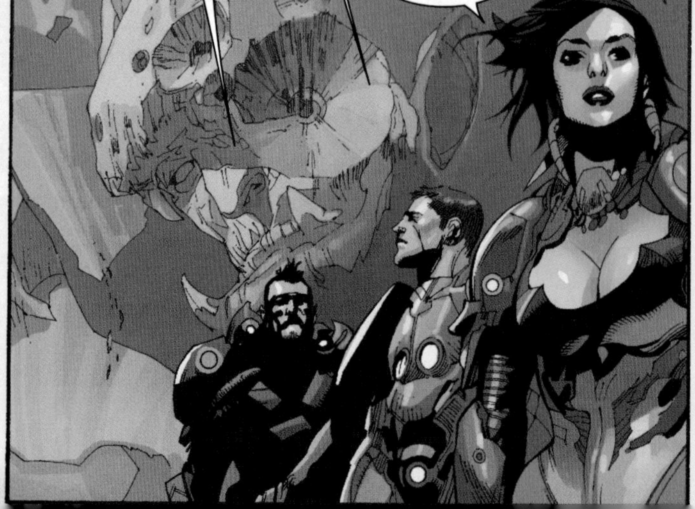
LET'S PLAN ON OPTION (A), NOT (B). I CAN HELP.
THIS, WE KNOW. WE SAW YOU--HULK--FIGHTING ATTUMA'S ARMY AND SAW IN YOU A POWERFUL ALLY.
Mara goes on to explain that, despite it being one of the world's great repositories of SORCEROUS ARTIFACTS, Lemuria's merely a STEPPING STONE for Attuma.
SOMEWHERE IN YOU.

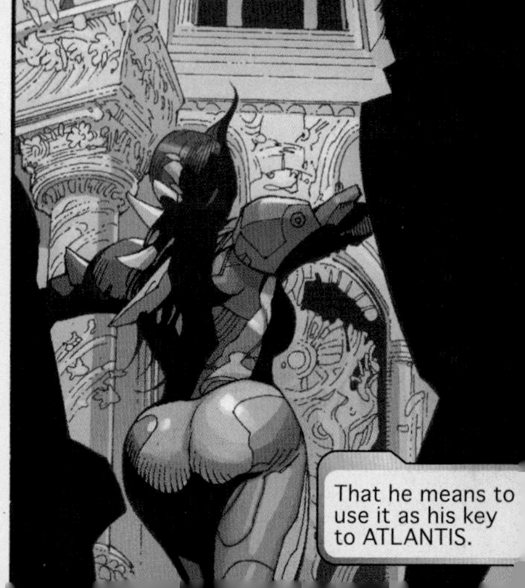
That it's Lemuria's ALCHEMISTS he coveted, not its SOLDIERS or its MAGIC. And that it's rumored they've INVENTED something for him.
That he means to use it as his key to ATLANTIS.

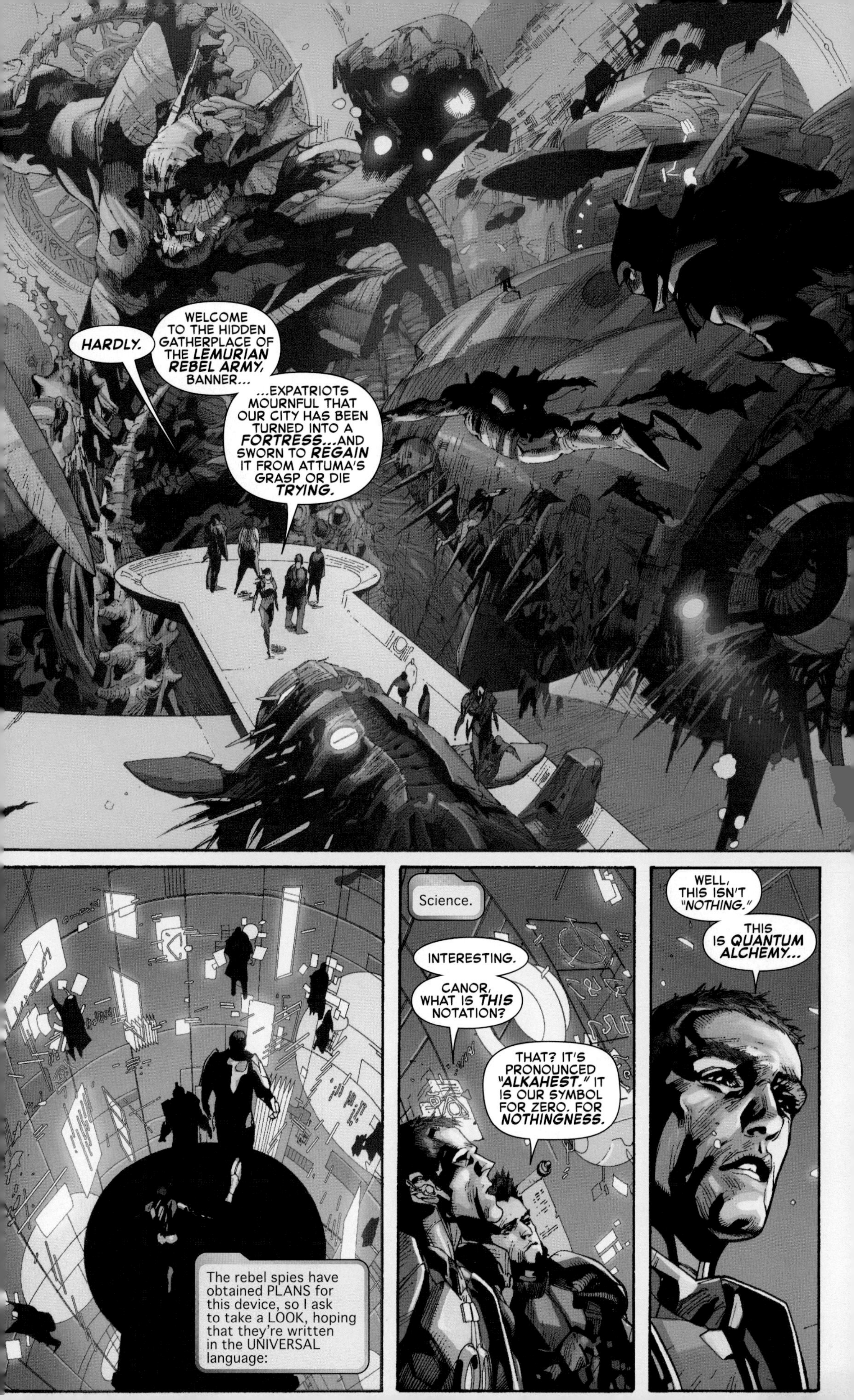
HARDLY.
WELCOME TO THE HIDDEN GATHERPLACE OF THE LEMURIAN REBEL ARMY, BANNER...
...EXPATRIOTS MOURNFUL THAT OUR CITY HAS BEEN TURNED INTO A FORTRESS...AND SWORN TO REGAIN IT FROM ATTUMA'S GRASP OR DIE TRYING.
The rebel spies have obtained PLANS for this device, so I ask to take a LOOK, hoping that they're written in the UNIVERSAL language:
Science.
INTERESTING.
CANOR, WHAT IS THIS NOTATION?
THAT? IT'S PRONOUNCED "ALKAHEST." IT IS OUR SYMBOL FOR ZERO. FOR NOTHINGNESS.
WELL, THIS ISN'T "NOTHING."
THIS IS QUANTUM ALCHEMY...

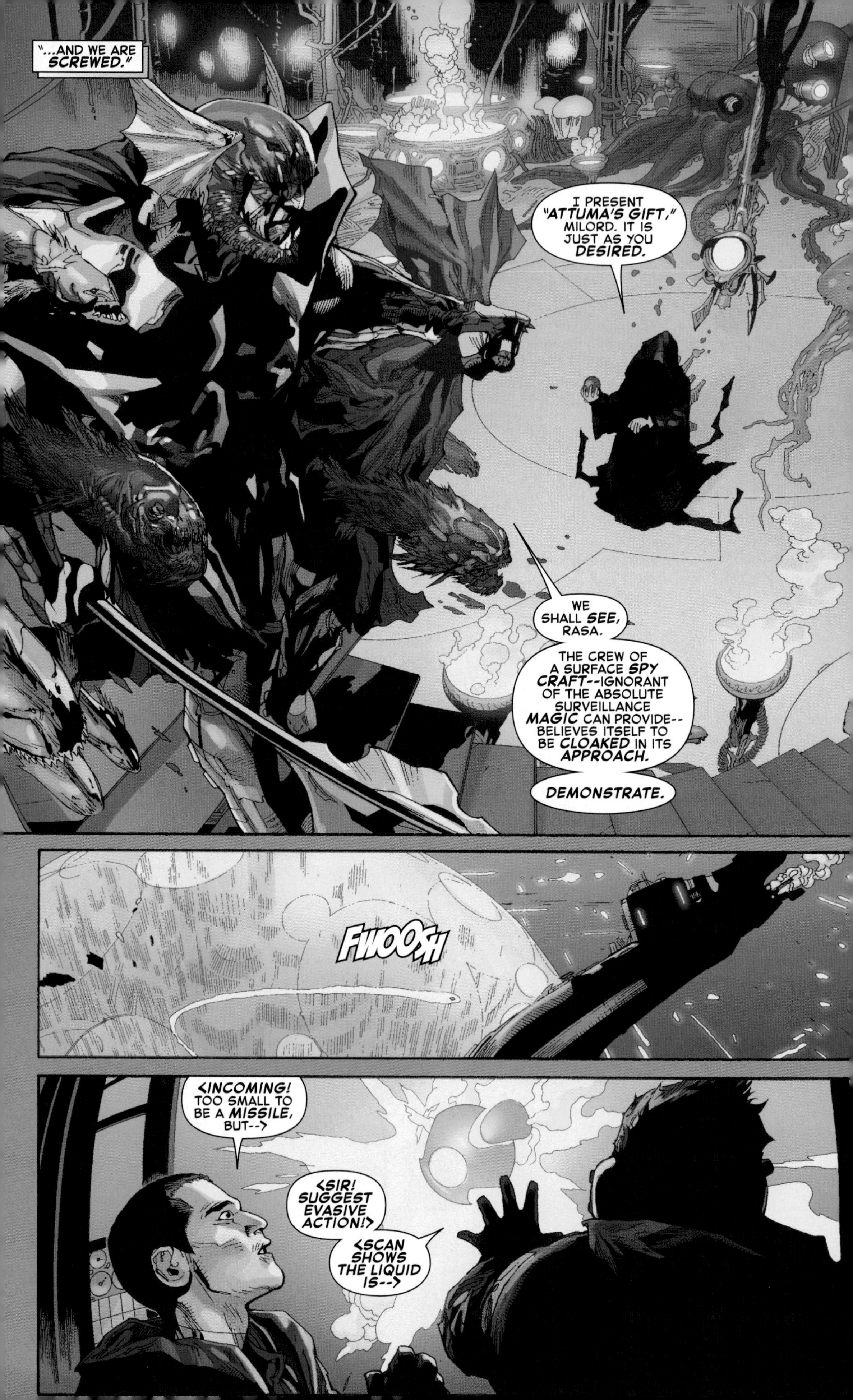
"...AND WE ARE SCREWED."
I PRESENT "ATTUMA'S GIFT," MILORD. IT IS JUST AS YOU DESIRED.
WE SHALL SEE, RASA.
THE CREW OF A SURFACE SPY CRAFT--IGNORANT OF THE ABSOLUTE SURVEILLANCE MAGIC CAN PROVIDE--BELIEVES ITSELF TO BE CLOAKED IN ITS APPROACH.
DEMONSTRATE.
FWOOSH
<INCOMING! TOO SMALL TO BE A MISSILE, BUT-->
<SIR! SUGGEST EVASIVE ACTION!>
<SCAN SHOWS THE LIQUID IS-->

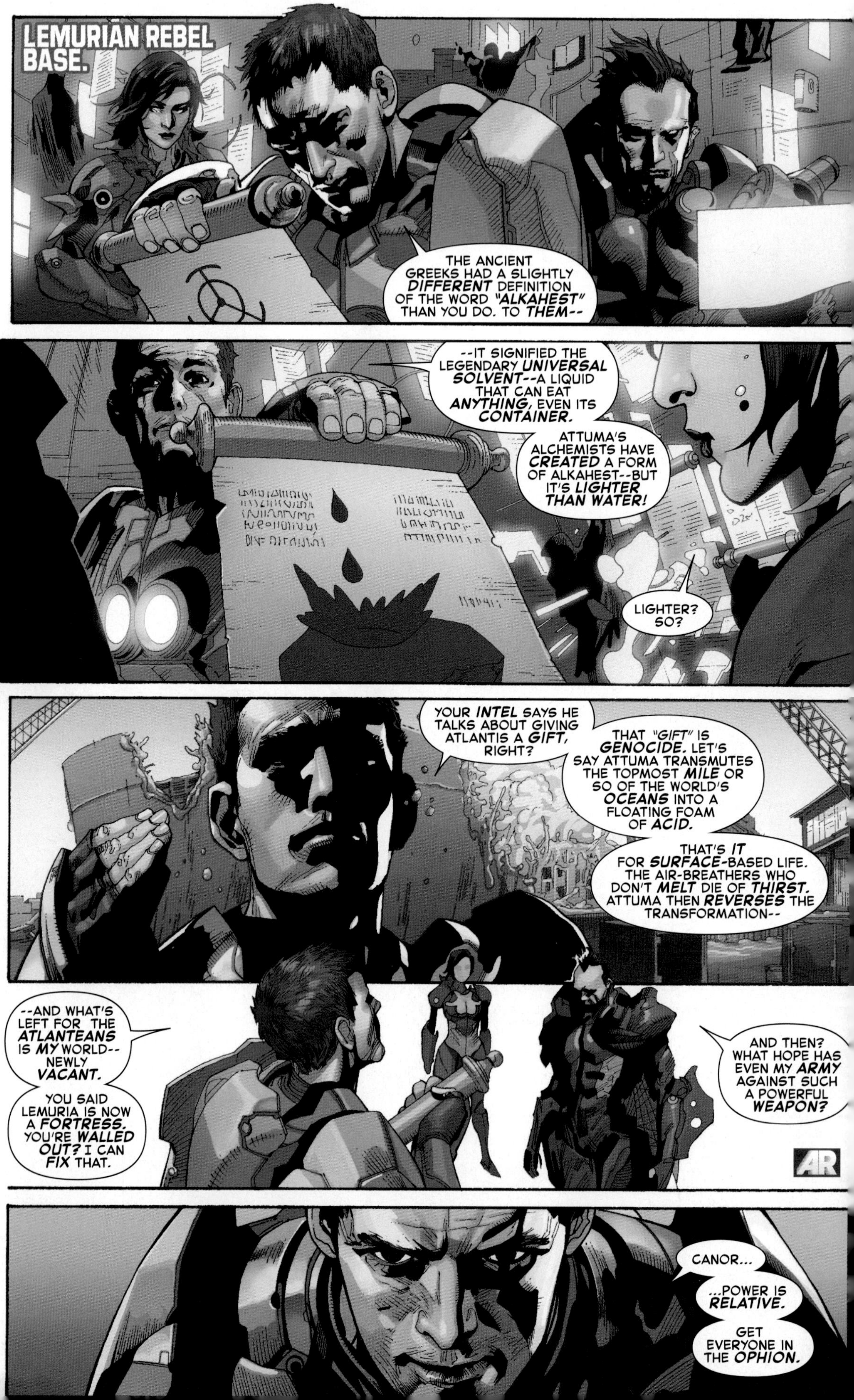
LEMURIAN REBEL BASE.
THE ANCIENT GREEKS HAD A SLIGHTLY DIFFERENT DEFINITION OF THE WORD "ALKAHEST" THAN YOU DO. TO THEM--
--IT SIGNIFIED THE LEGENDARY UNIVERSAL SOLVENT--A LIQUID THAT CAN EAT ANYTHING, EVEN ITS CONTAINER.
ATTUMA'S ALCHEMISTS HAVE CREATED A FORM OF ALKAHEST--BUT IT'S LIGHTER THAN WATER!
LIGHTER? SO?
YOUR INTEL SAYS HE TALKS ABOUT GIVING ATLANTIS A GIFT, RIGHT?
THAT "GIFT" IS GENOCIDE. LET'S SAY ATTUMA TRANSMUTES THE TOPMOST MILE OR SO OF THE WORLD'S OCEANS INTO A FLOATING FOAM OF ACID.
THAT'S IT FOR SURFACE-BASED LIFE. THE AIR-BREATHERS WHO DON'T MELT DIE OF THIRST. ATTUMA THEN REVERSES THE TRANSFORMATION--
--AND WHAT'S LEFT FOR THE ATLANTEANS IS MY WORLD--NEWLY VACANT.
YOU SAID LEMURIA IS NOW A FORTRESS. YOU'RE WALLED OUT? I CAN FIX THAT.
AND THEN? WHAT HOPE HAS EVEN MY ARMY AGAINST SUCH A POWERFUL WEAPON?
AR
CANOR...
...POWER IS RELATIVE.
GET EVERYONE IN THE OPHION.

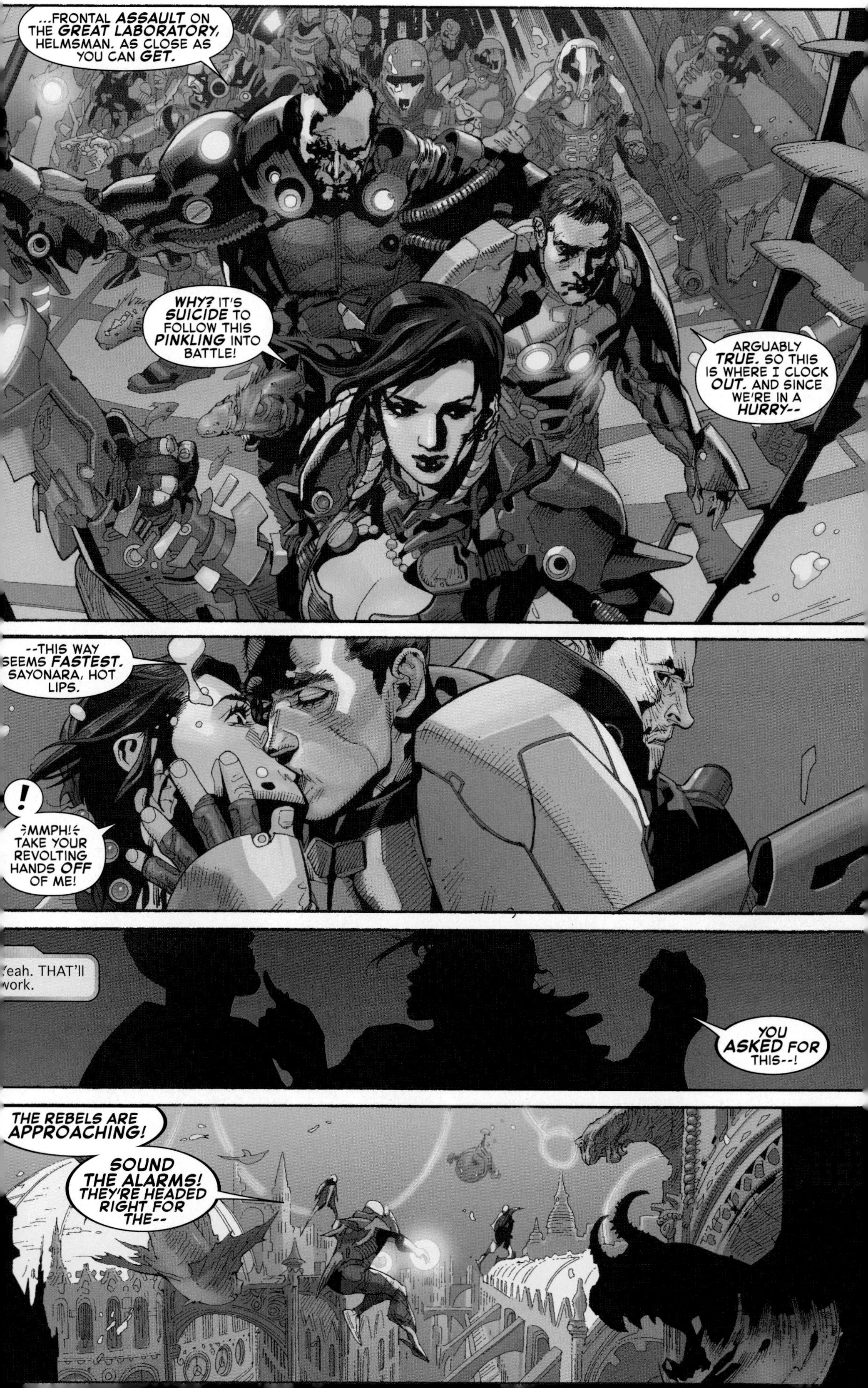
...FRONTAL ASSAULT ON THE GREAT LABORATORY, HELMSMAN. AS CLOSE AS YOU CAN GET.
WHY? IT'S SUICIDE TO FOLLOW THIS PINKLING INTO BATTLE!
ARGUABLY TRUE. SO THIS IS WHERE I CLOCK OUT. AND SINCE WE'RE IN A HURRY--
--THIS WAY SEEMS FASTEST. SAYONARA, HOT LIPS.
!
MMPH! TAKE YOUR REVOLTING HANDS OFF OF ME!
Yeah. THAT'll work.
YOU ASKED FOR THIS--!
THE REBELS ARE APPROACHING!
SOUND THE ALARMS! THEY'RE HEADED RIGHT FOR THE--

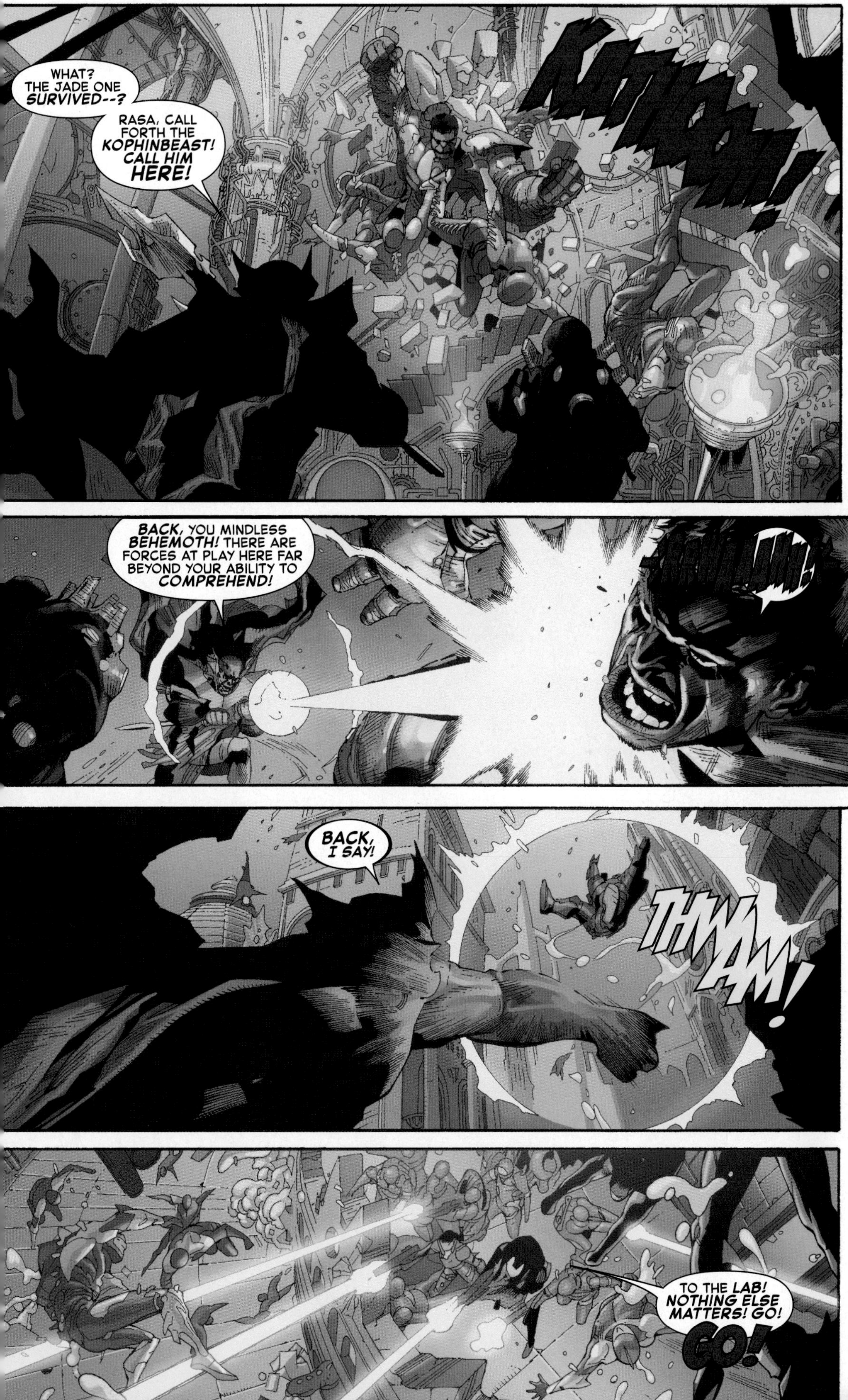
WHAT? THE JADE ONE SURVIVED--?
RASA, CALL FORTH THE KOPHINBEAST! CALL HIM HERE!
BACK, YOU MINDLESS BEHEMOTH! THERE ARE FORCES AT PLAY HERE FAR BEYOND YOUR ABILITY TO COMPREHEND!
BACK, I SAY!
THWAAM!
TO THE LAB! NOTHING ELSE MATTERS! GO! GO!

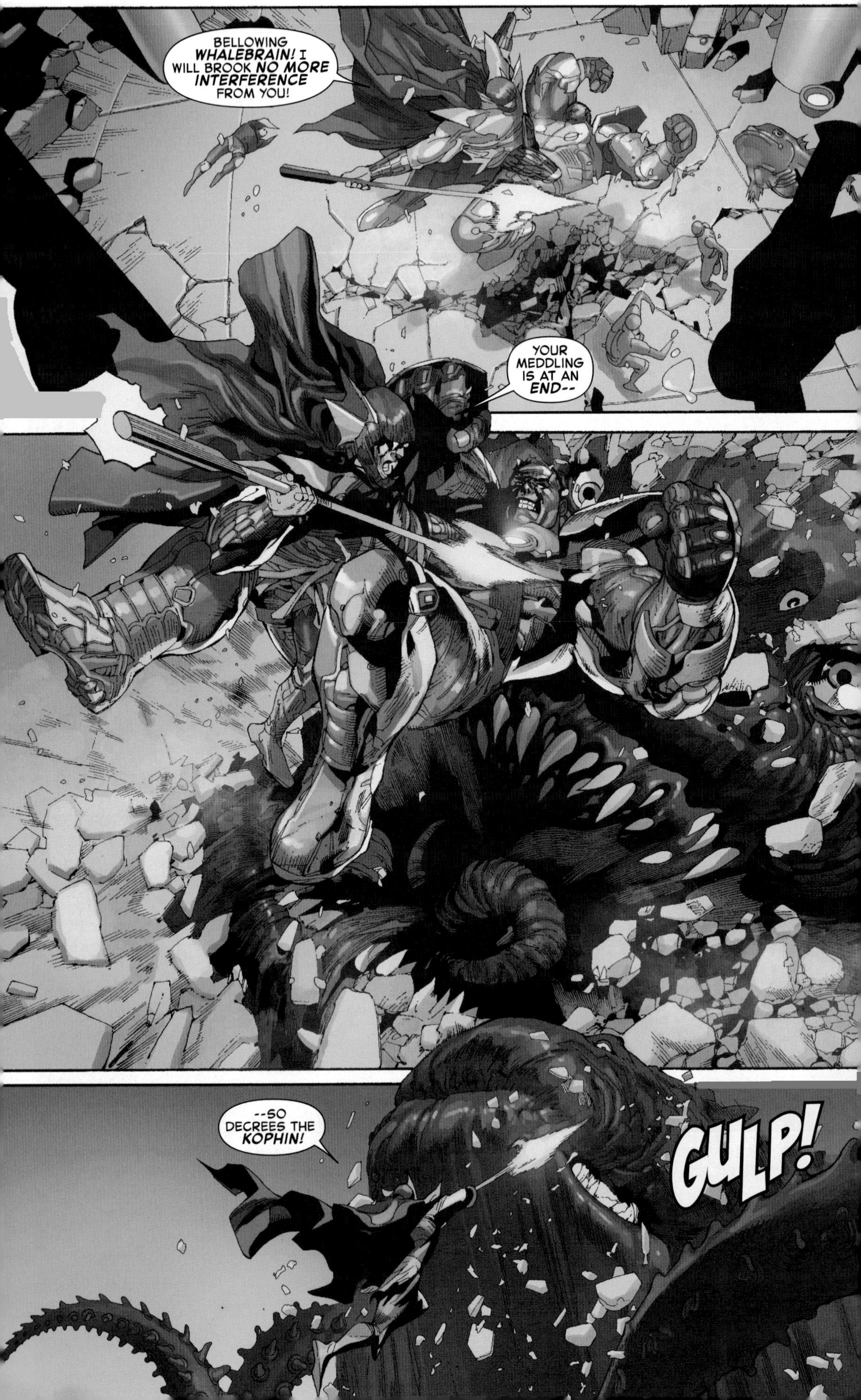
BELLOWING WHALEBRAIN! I WILL BROOK NO MORE INTERFERENCE FROM YOU!
YOUR MEDDLING IS AT AN END--
--SO DECREES THE KOPHIN!
GULP!

ATTUMA'S MEN CANNOT *HOLD* US!

IT IS NOT HIS *WARRIORS* WE MUST *FEAR*, CANOR--

--IT IS ATTUMA, *HIMSELF!* THE *GREEN MAN* WAS OUR DEFENSE AGAINST *HIM*--

--BUT *WHERE IS HE?*

FAST-DECAYING INSIDE THE BELLY OF THE MYSTICAL *KOPHIN*, THAT'S WHERE!

HE STRUGGLES FOR *NAUGHT!*

GO AHEAD! TRY TO CARVE HIS *RELEASE!* YOU *CANNOT!* IT IS WHAT MAKES THIS THE GREATEST TRAP OF *ALL!*

THE HIDE OF THE *KOPHIN* IS MAGICALLY *IMPENETRABLE!* NOTHING CAN TEAR *THROUGH* IT! NO--

--THING--

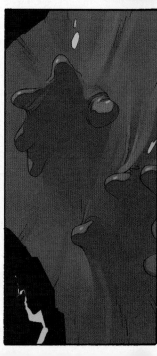

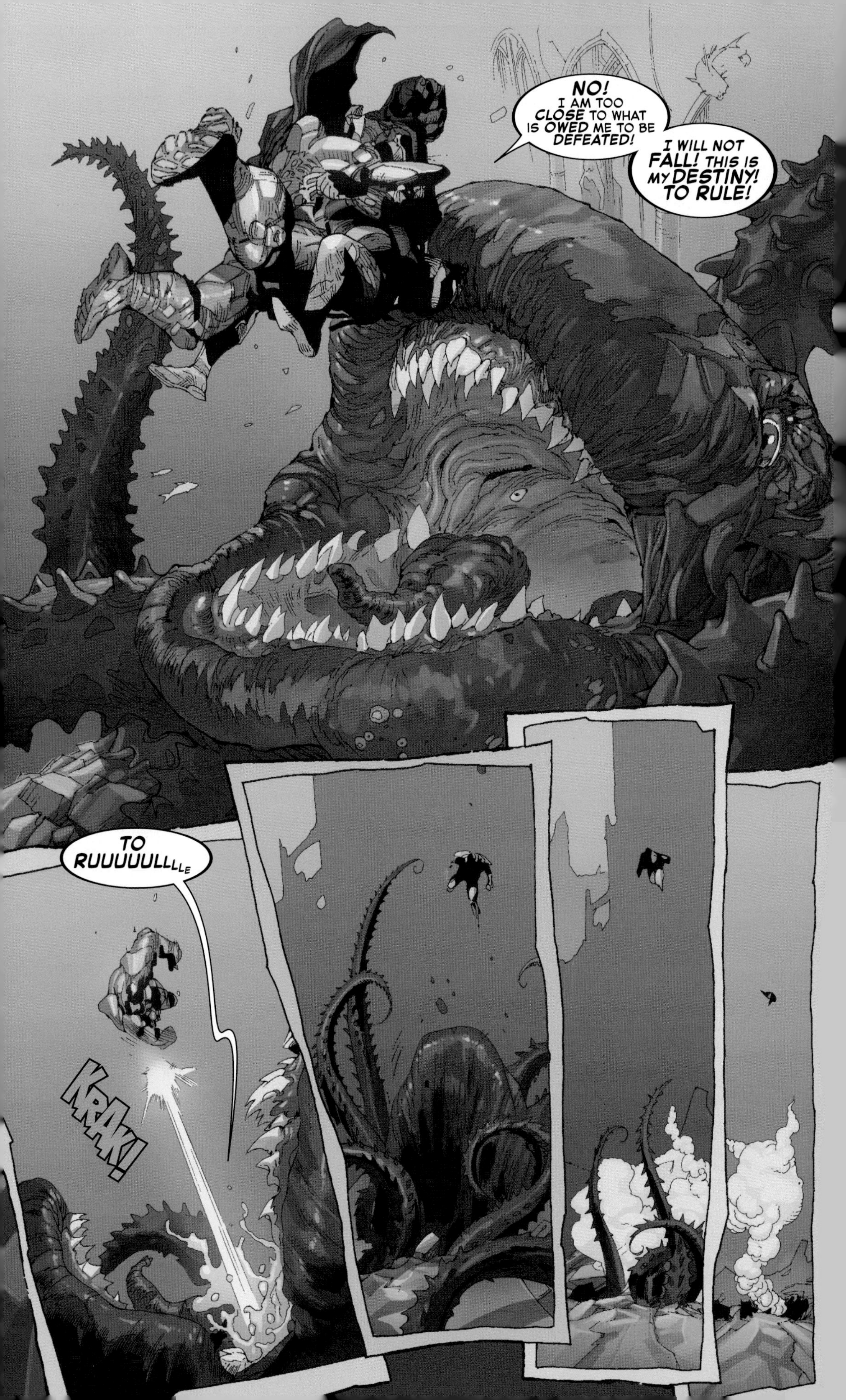
NO! I AM TOO CLOSE TO WHAT IS OWED ME TO BE DEFEATED!
I WILL NOT FALL! THIS IS MY DESTINY! TO RULE!
TO RUUUUULLLLE
KRAK!

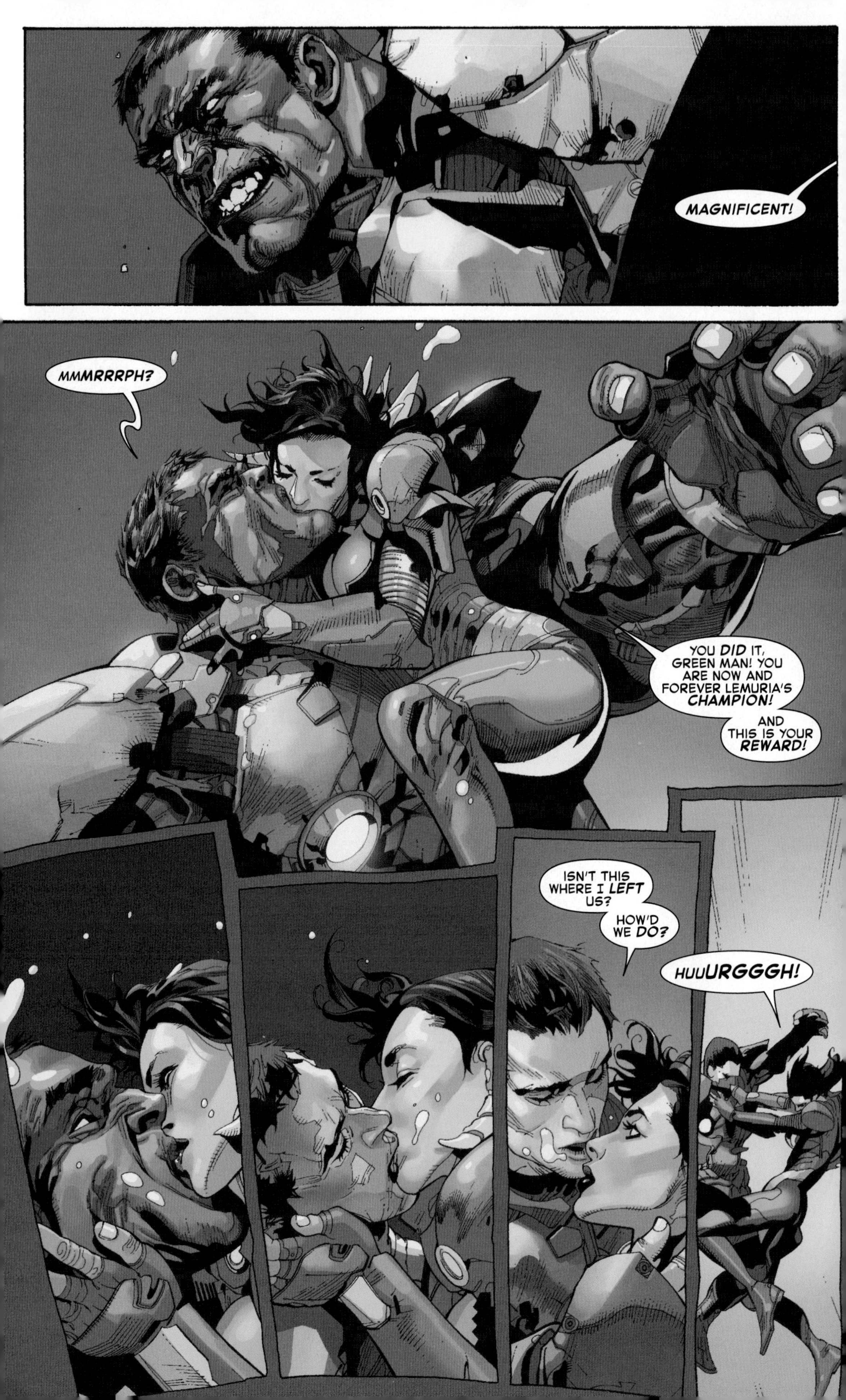
MAGNIFICENT!
MMMRRRPH?
YOU DID IT, GREEN MAN! YOU ARE NOW AND FOREVER LEMURIA'S CHAMPION!
AND THIS IS YOUR REWARD!
ISN'T THIS WHERE I LEFT US?
HOW'D WE DO?
HUUURGGGH!

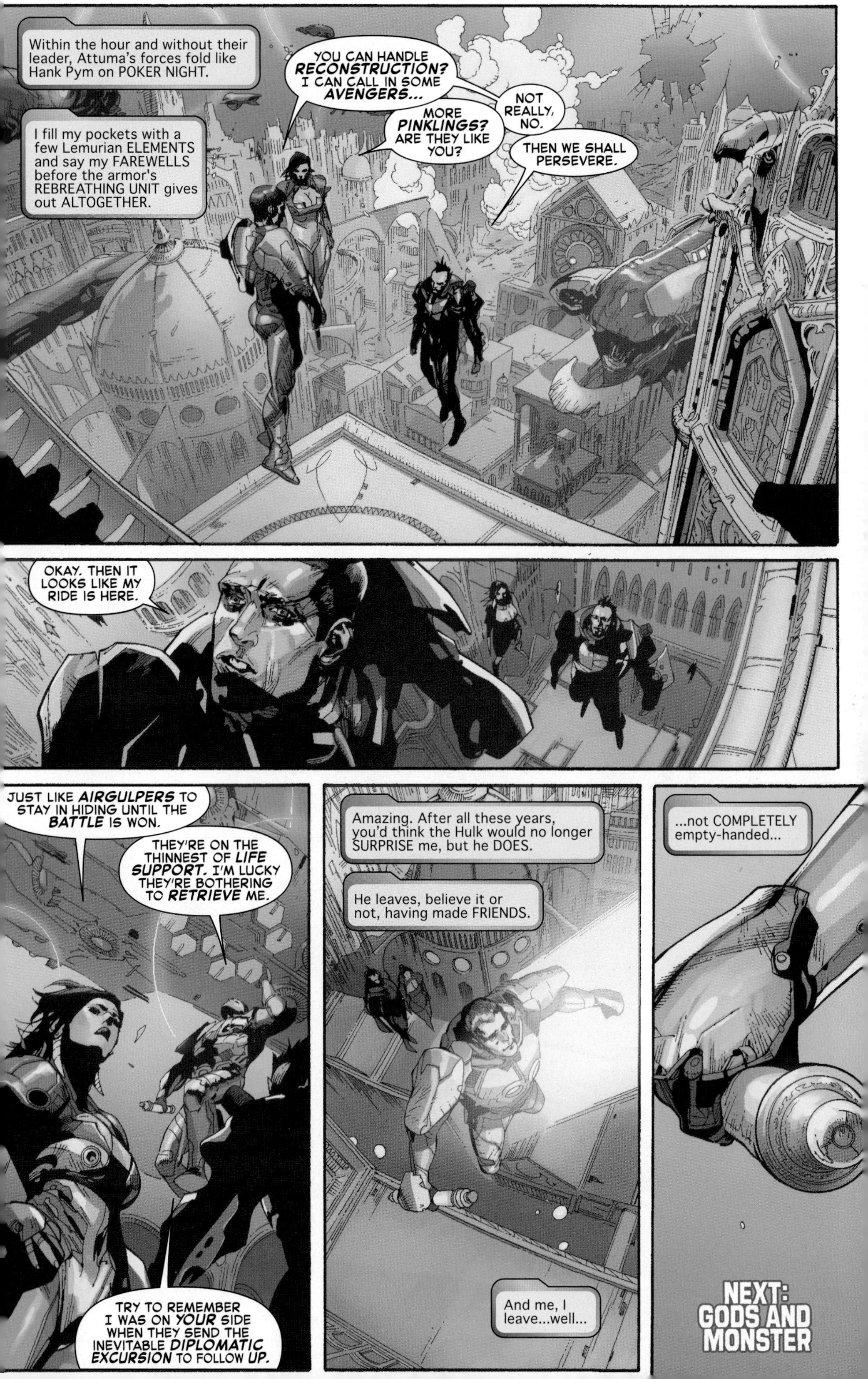

Within the hour and without their leader, Attuma's forces fold like Hank Pym on POKER NIGHT.
I fill my pockets with a few Lemurian ELEMENTS and say my FAREWELLS before the armor's REBREATHING UNIT gives out ALTOGETHER.
YOU CAN HANDLE RECONSTRUCTION? I CAN CALL IN SOME AVENGERS...
MORE PINKLINGS? ARE THEY LIKE YOU?
NOT REALLY, NO.
THEN WE SHALL PERSEVERE.
OKAY. THEN IT LOOKS LIKE MY RIDE IS HERE.
JUST LIKE AIRGULPERS TO STAY IN HIDING UNTIL THE BATTLE IS WON.
THEY'RE ON THE THINNEST OF LIFE SUPPORT. I'M LUCKY THEY'RE BOTHERING TO RETRIEVE ME.
TRY TO REMEMBER I WAS ON YOUR SIDE WHEN THEY SEND THE INEVITABLE DIPLOMATIC EXCURSION TO FOLLOW UP.
Amazing. After all these years, you'd think the Hulk would no longer SURPRISE me, but he DOES.
He leaves, believe it or not, having made FRIENDS.
And me, I leave...well...
...not COMPLETELY empty-handed...
NEXT: GODS AND MONSTER

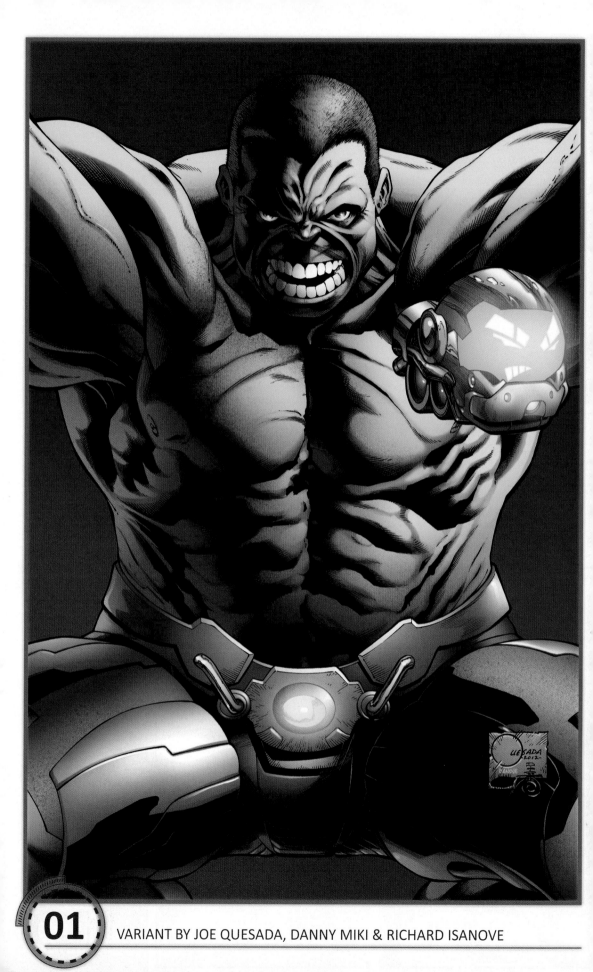

01

VARIANT BY JOE QUESADA, DANNY MIKI & RICHARD ISANOVE

SKETCH VARIANT BY JOE QUESADA & DANNY MIKI

01

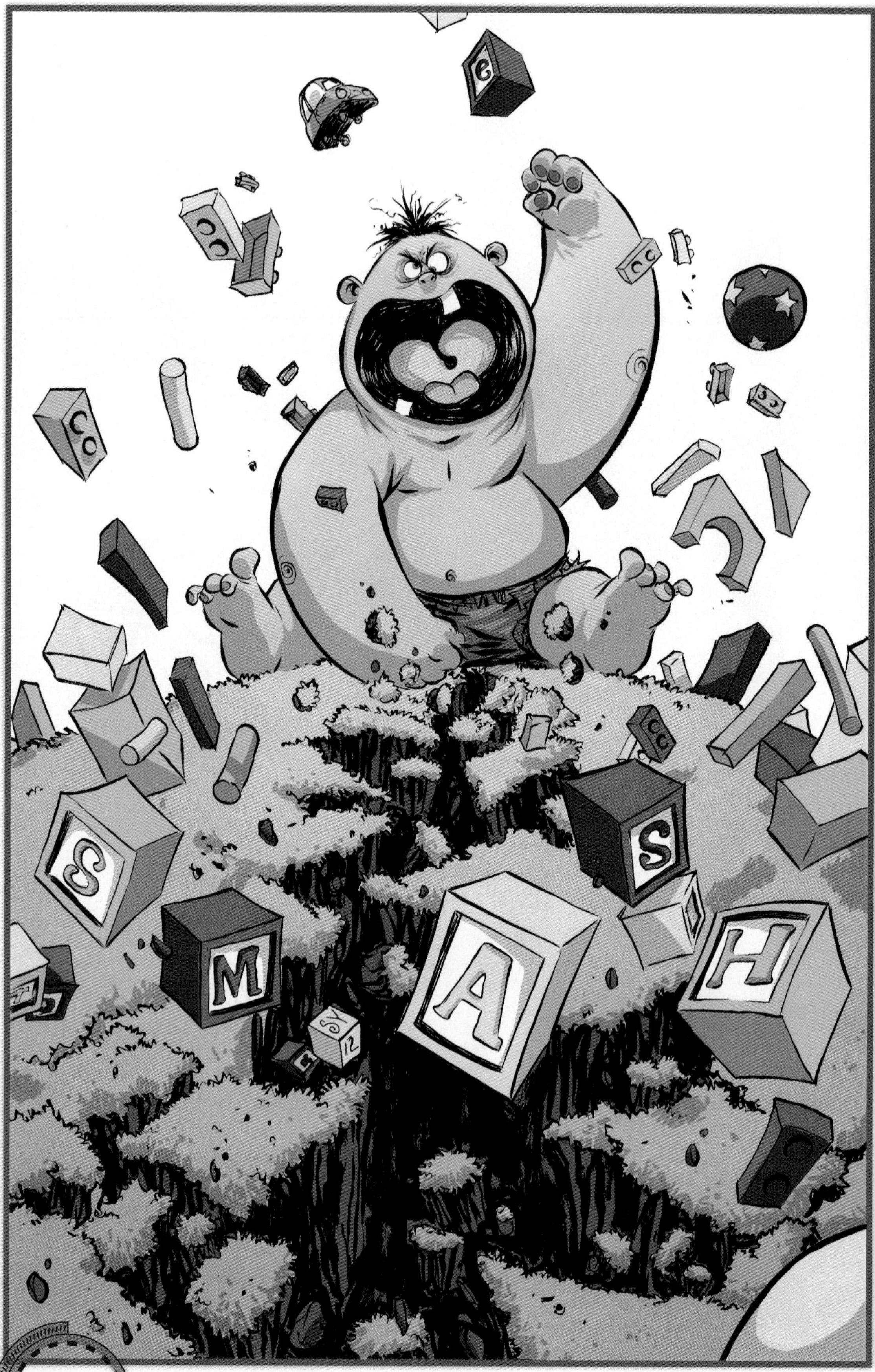
S
M
A
S
H

01

VARIANT BY SKOTTIE YOUNG

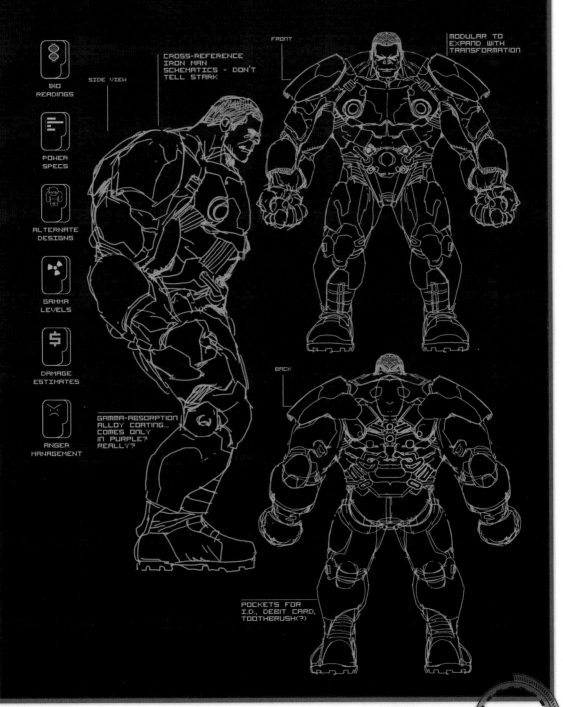

BIO
READINGS

POWER
SPECS

ALTERNATE
DESIGNS

GAMMA
LEVELS

DAMAGE
ESTIMATES

ANGER
MANAGEMENT

SIDE VIEW

CROSS-REFERENCE
IRON MAN
SCHEMATICS - DON'T
TELL STARK

FRONT

MODULAR TO
EXPAND WITH
TRANSFORMATION

BACK

GAMMA-ABSORPTION
ALLOY COATING...
COMES ONLY
IN PURPLE?
REALLY?

POCKETS FOR
I.D., DEBIT CARD,
TOOTHBRUSH(?)

VARIANT BY LEINIL FRANCIS YU

01

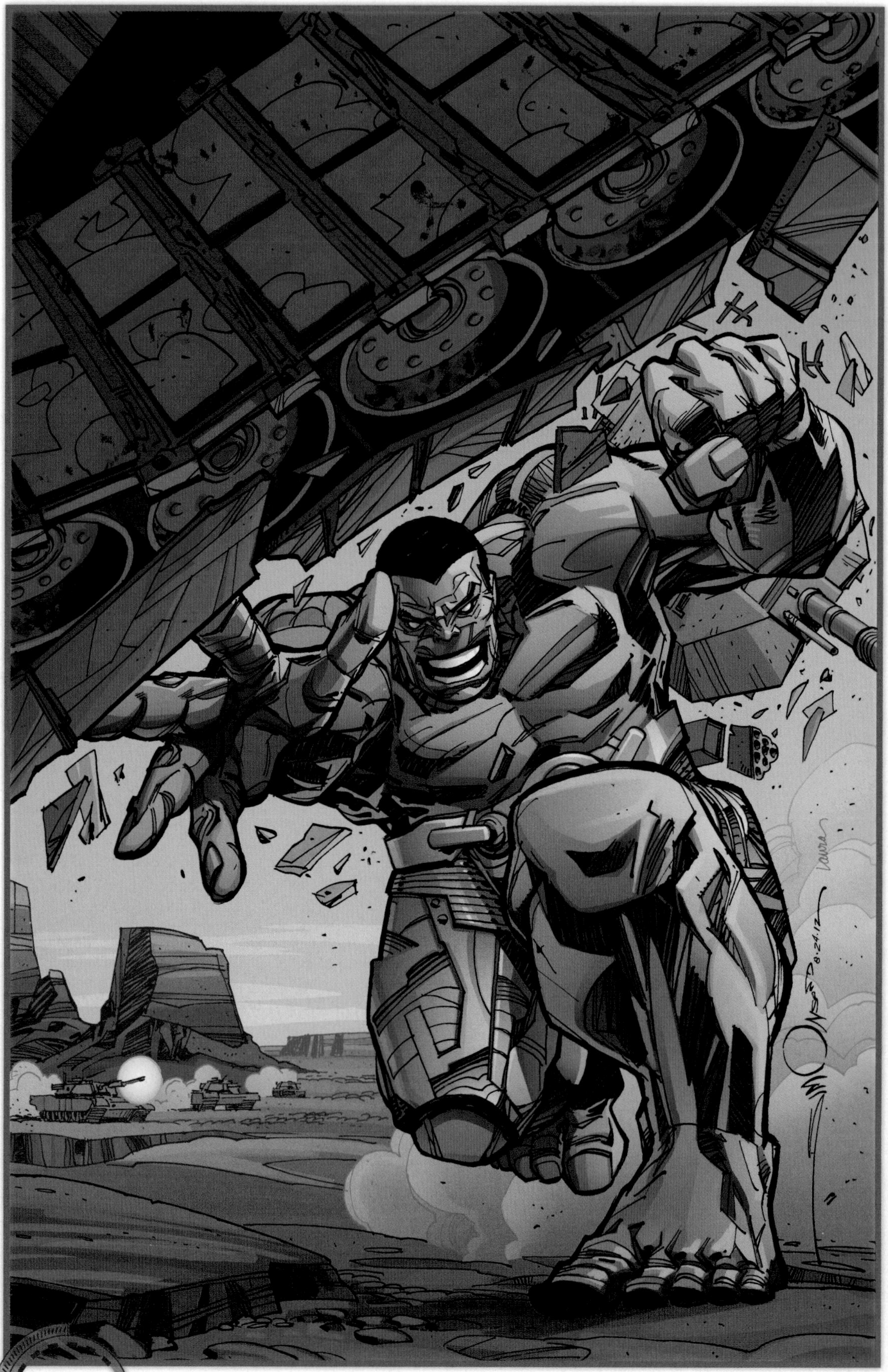

01 VARIANT BY WALTER SIMONSON & LAURA MARTIN

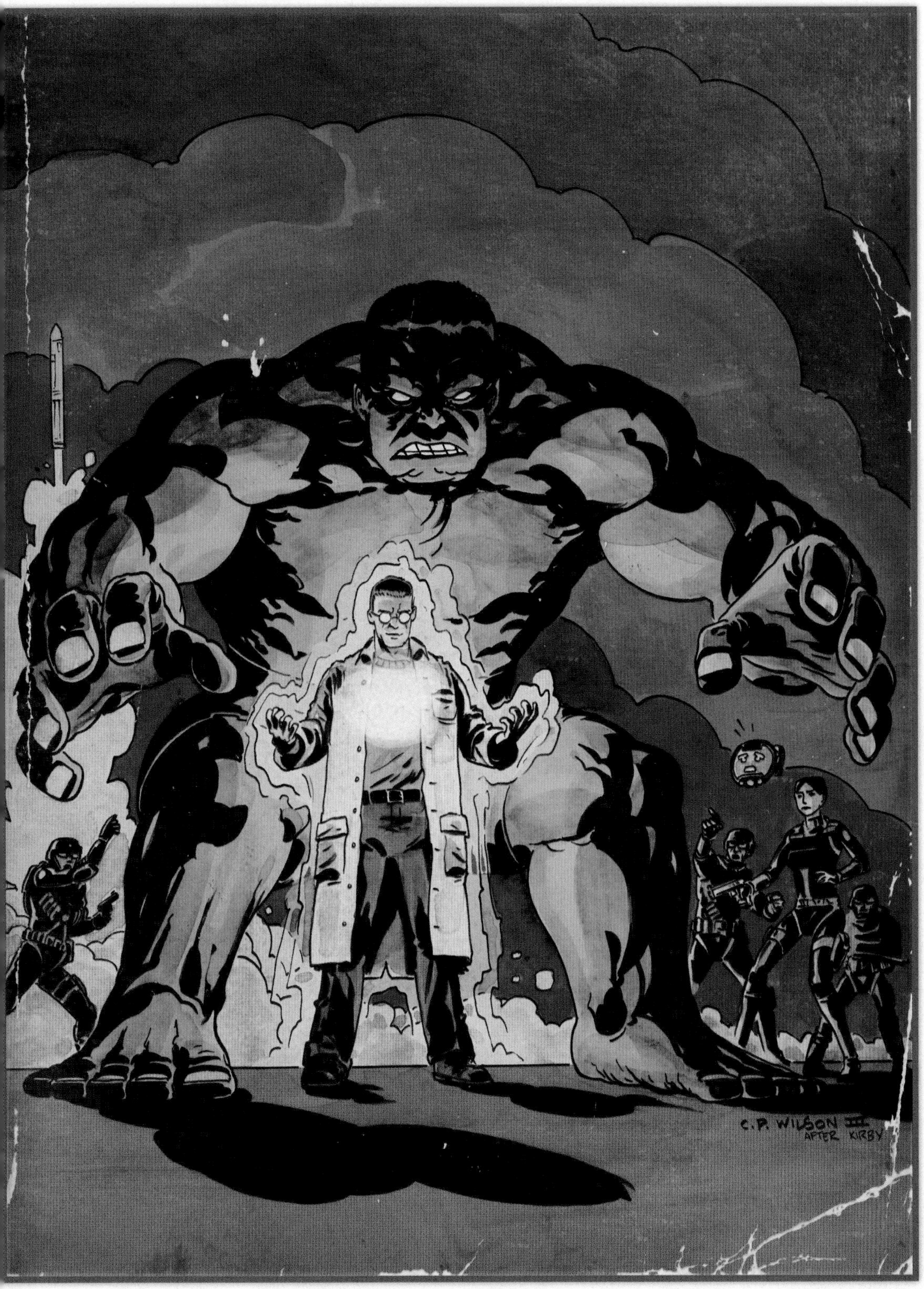
C.P. WILSON III
AFTER KIRBY

PHANTOM VARIANT BY C.P. WILSON III

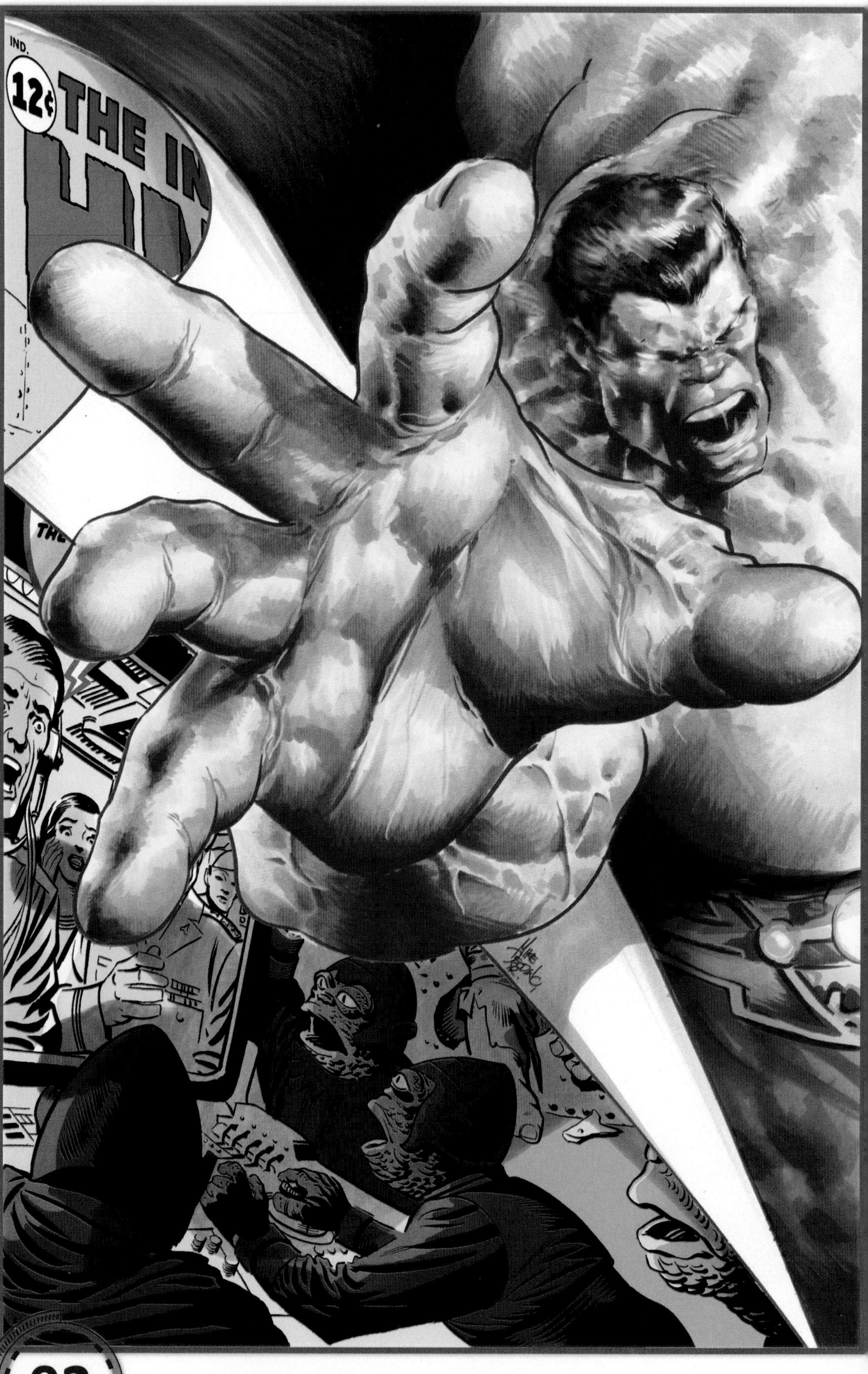
IND.
12¢ THE IN

 VARIANT BY MIKE DEODATO & RAIN BEREDO

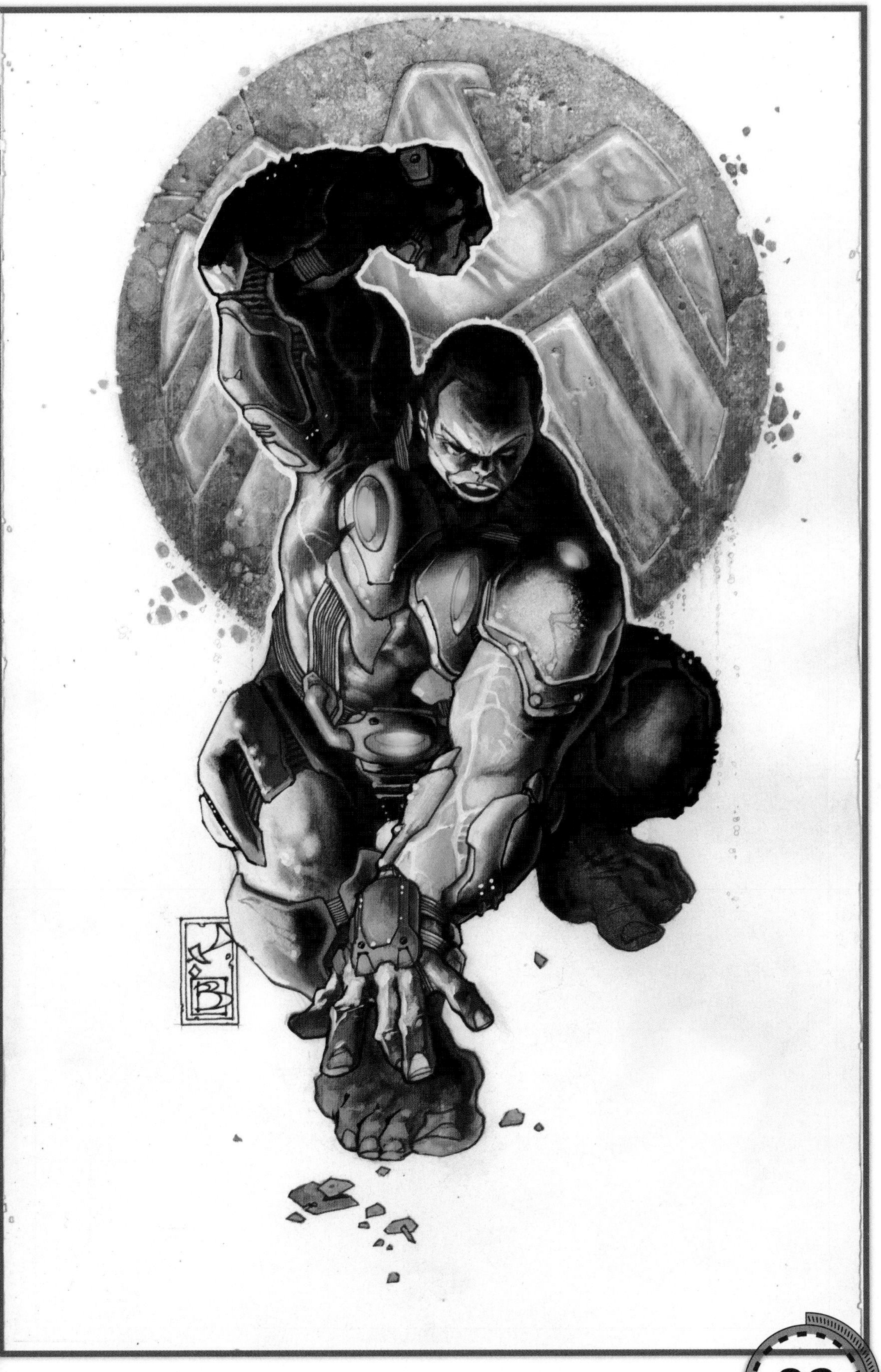

VARIANT BY SIMONE BIANCHI

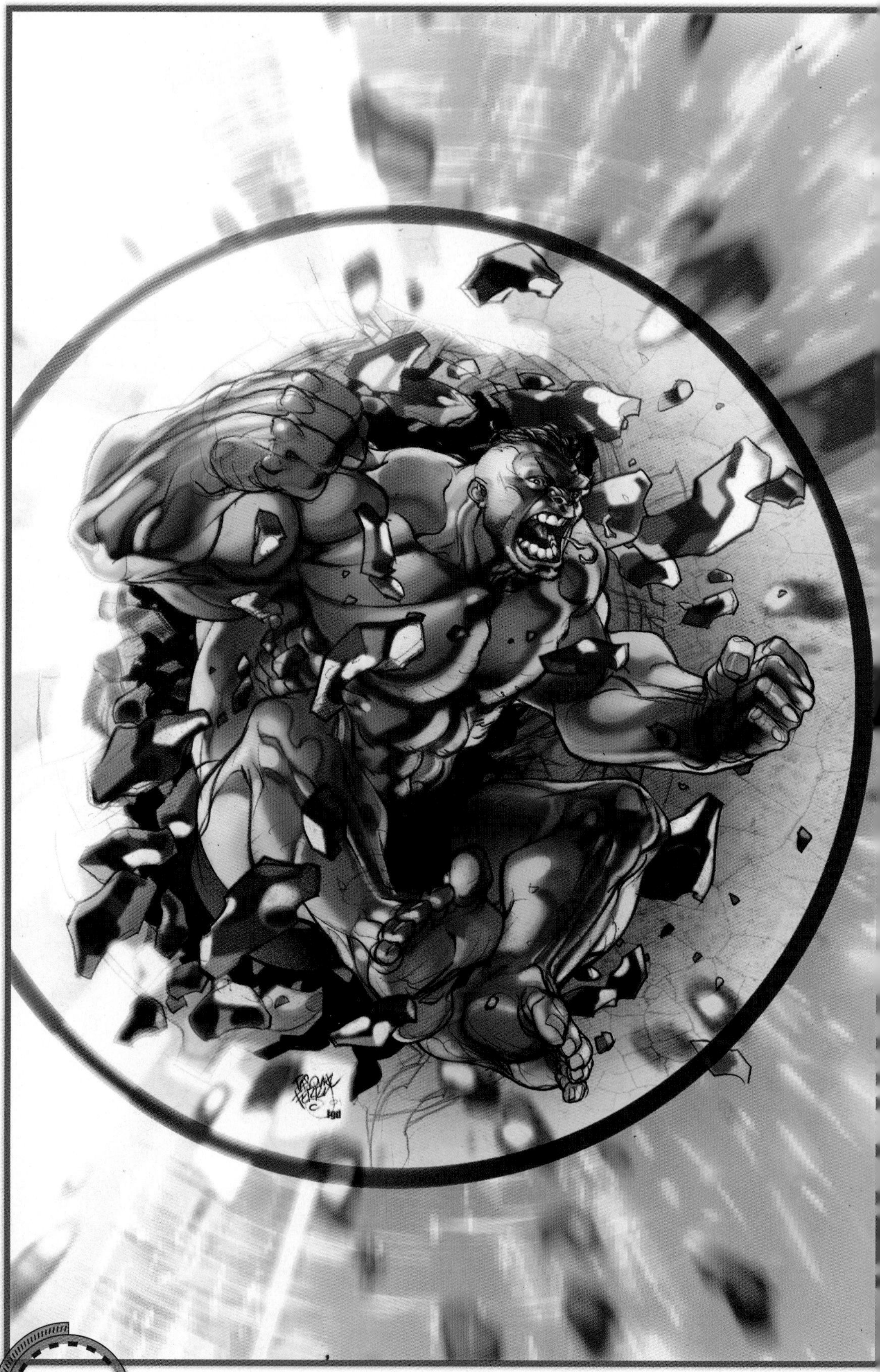

04

VARIANT BY PASQUAL FERRY & FRANK D'ARMATA

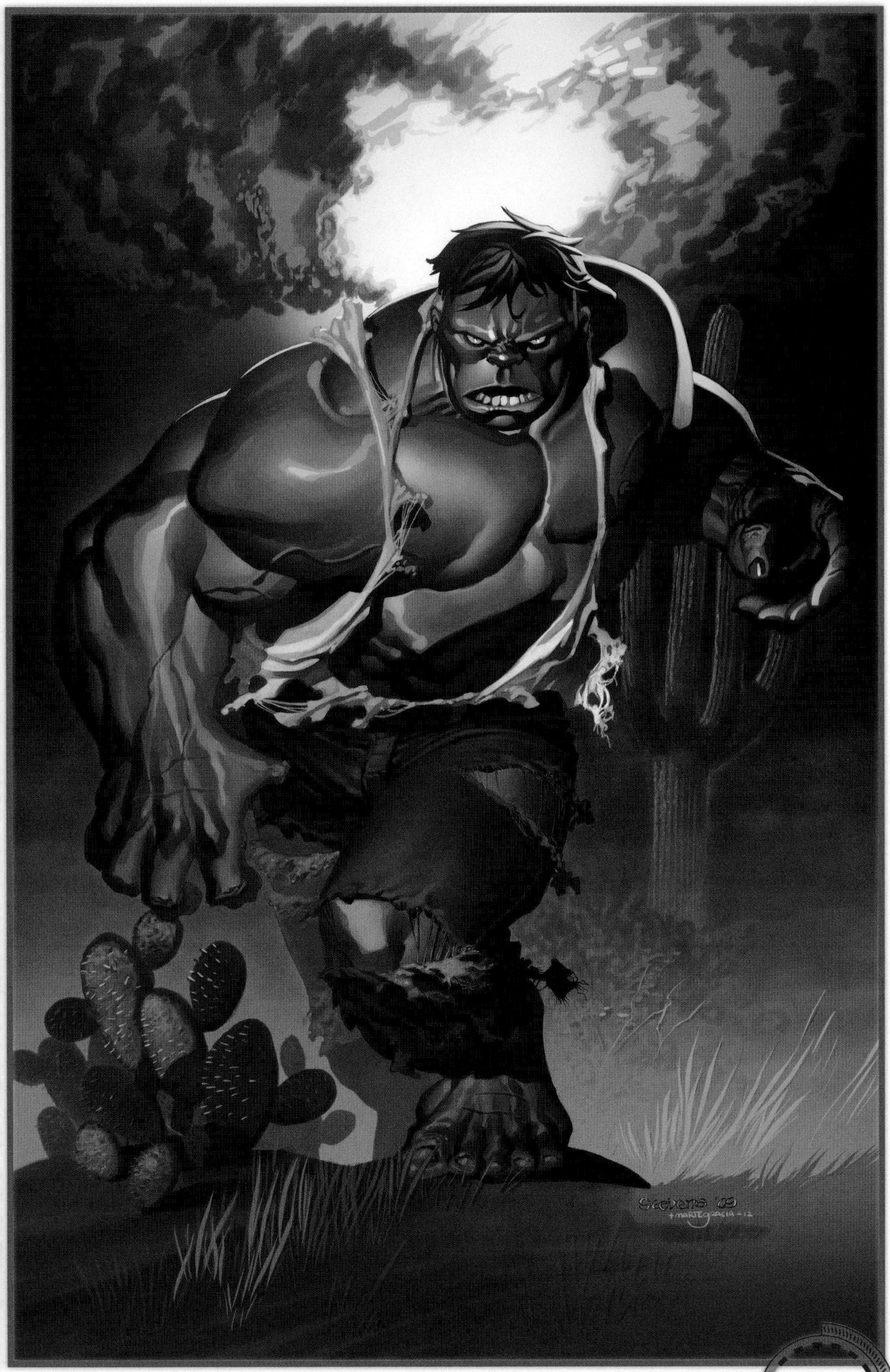

VARIANT BY CHRIS STEVENS & MARTE GRACIA

05

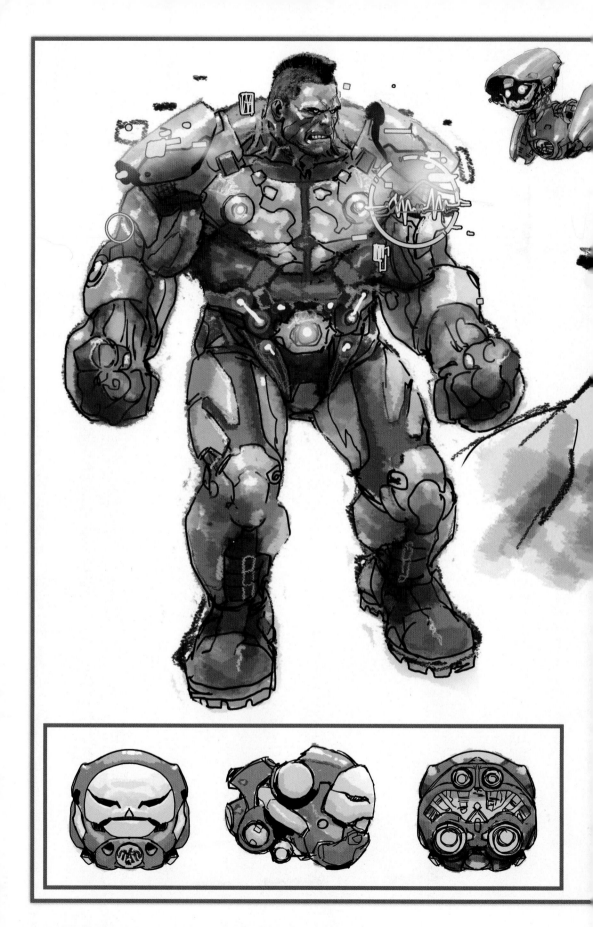

HULK AND R.O.B. CHARACTER STUDIES BY LEINIL FRANCIS YU

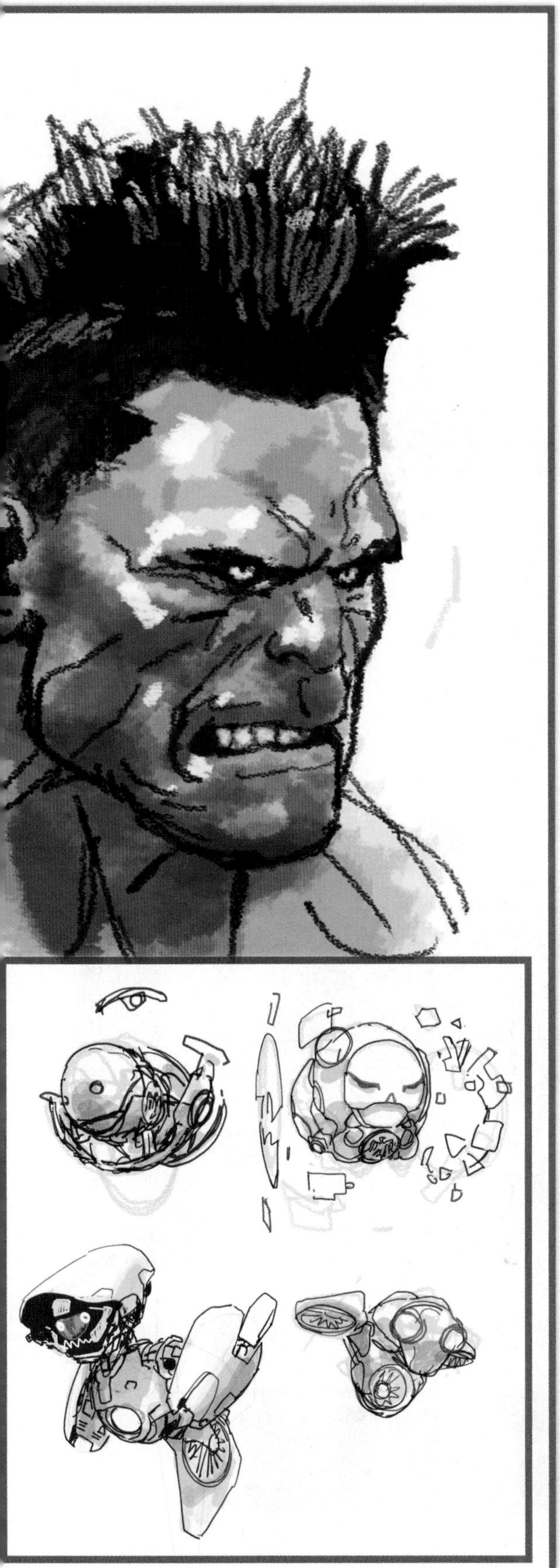
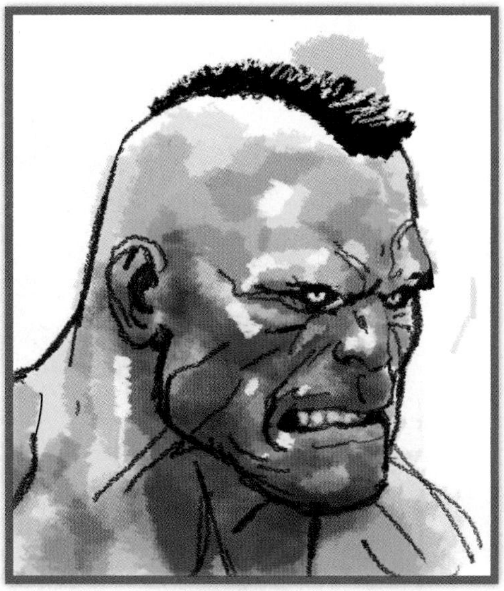
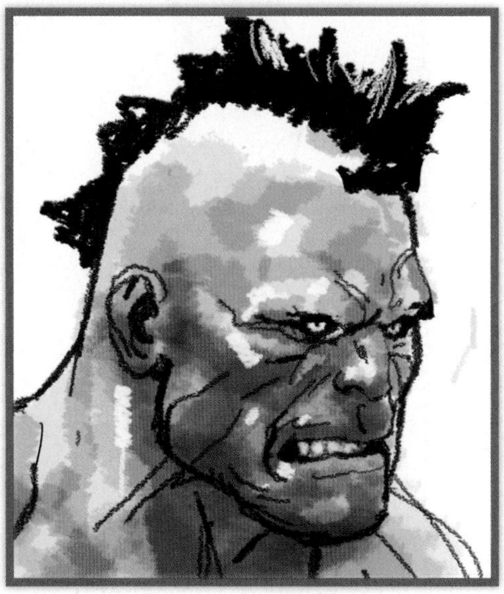
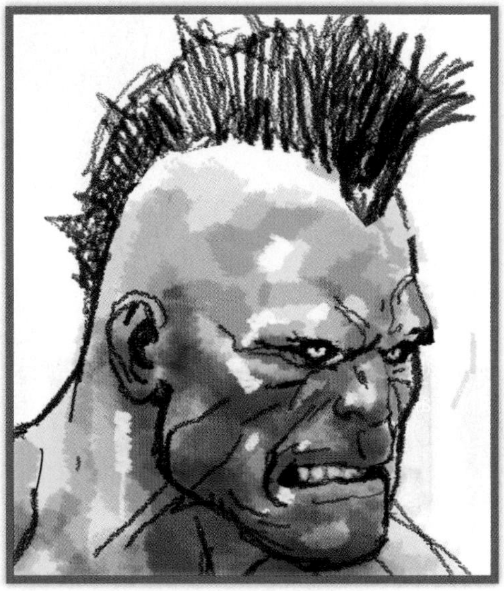

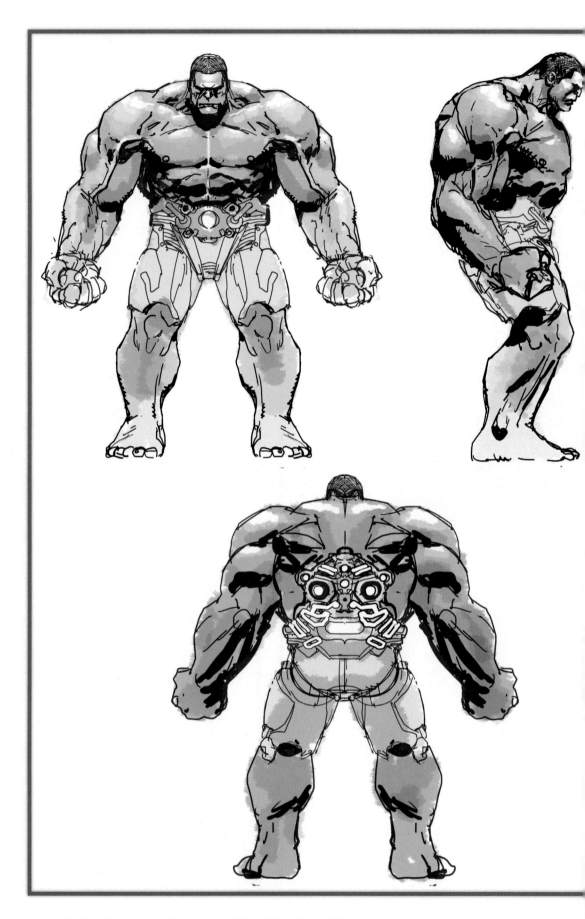

HULK ARMOR TURNAROUNDS BY LEINIL FRANCIS YU

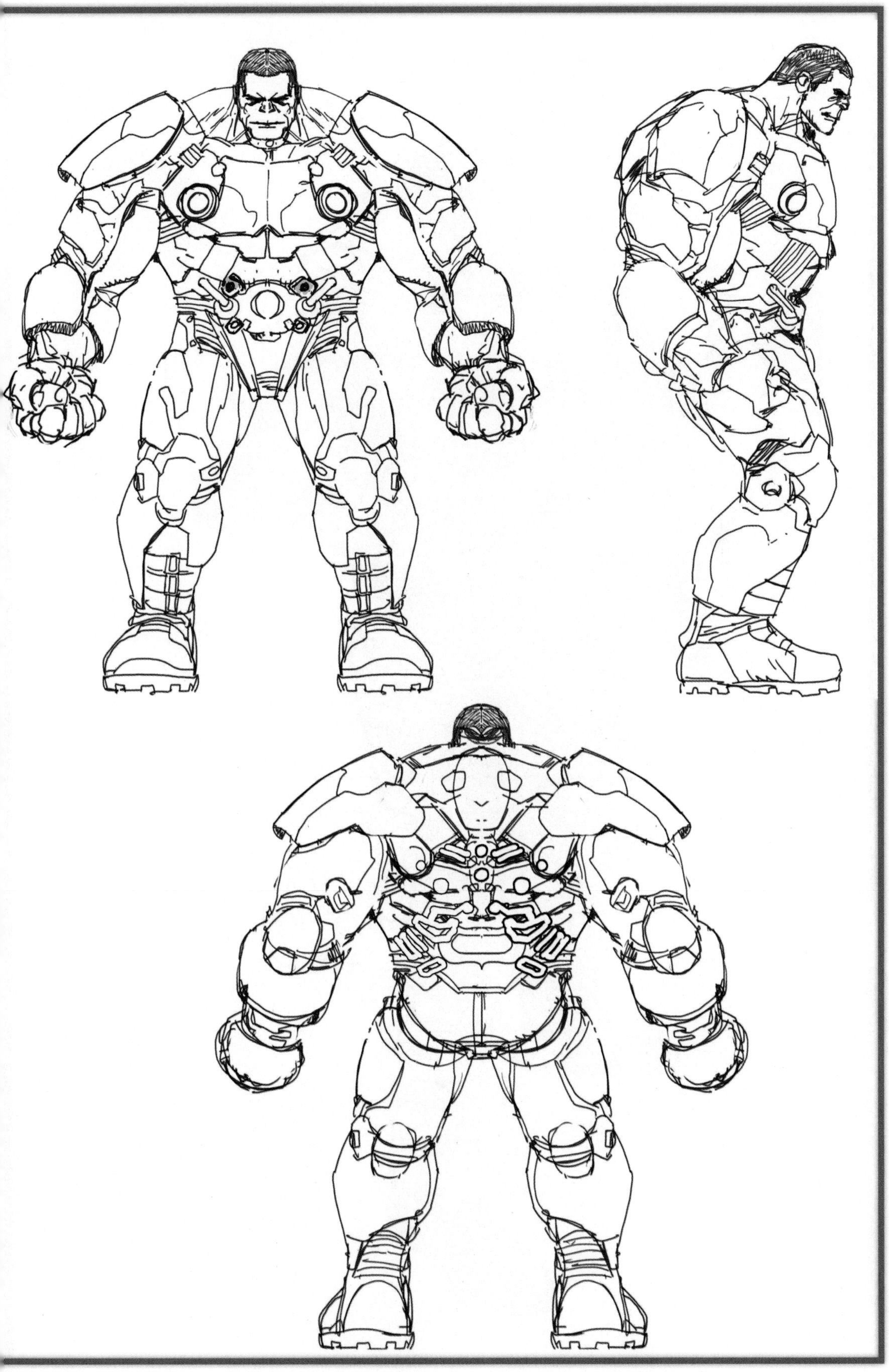

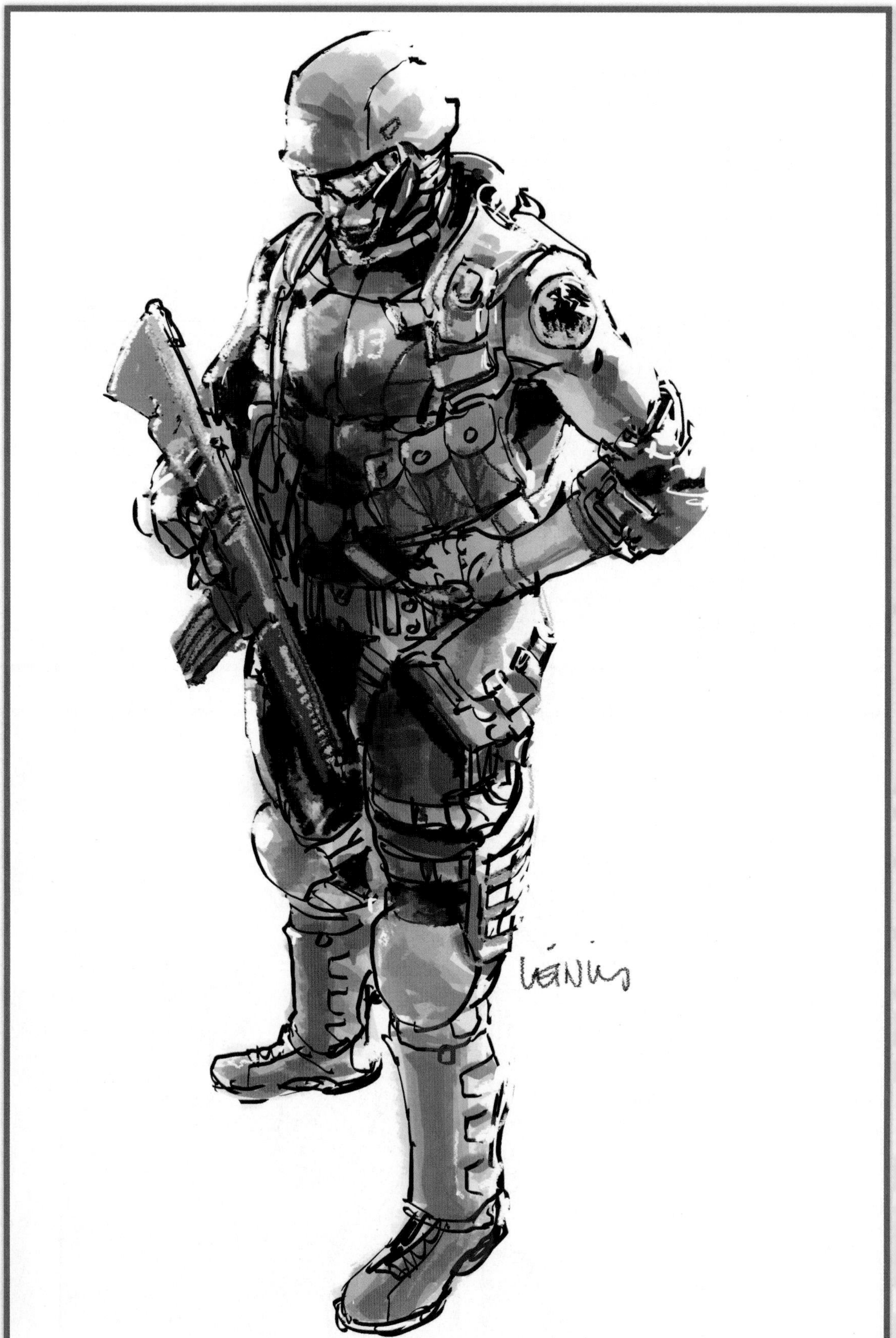
LEINIL

S.H.I.E.L.D. SOLDIER CHARACTER STUDY BY LEINIL FRANCIS YU

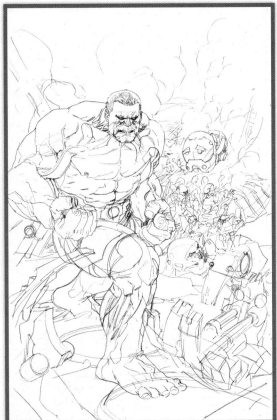

ISSUE #1 COVER ART PROCESS BY LEINIL FRANCIS YU

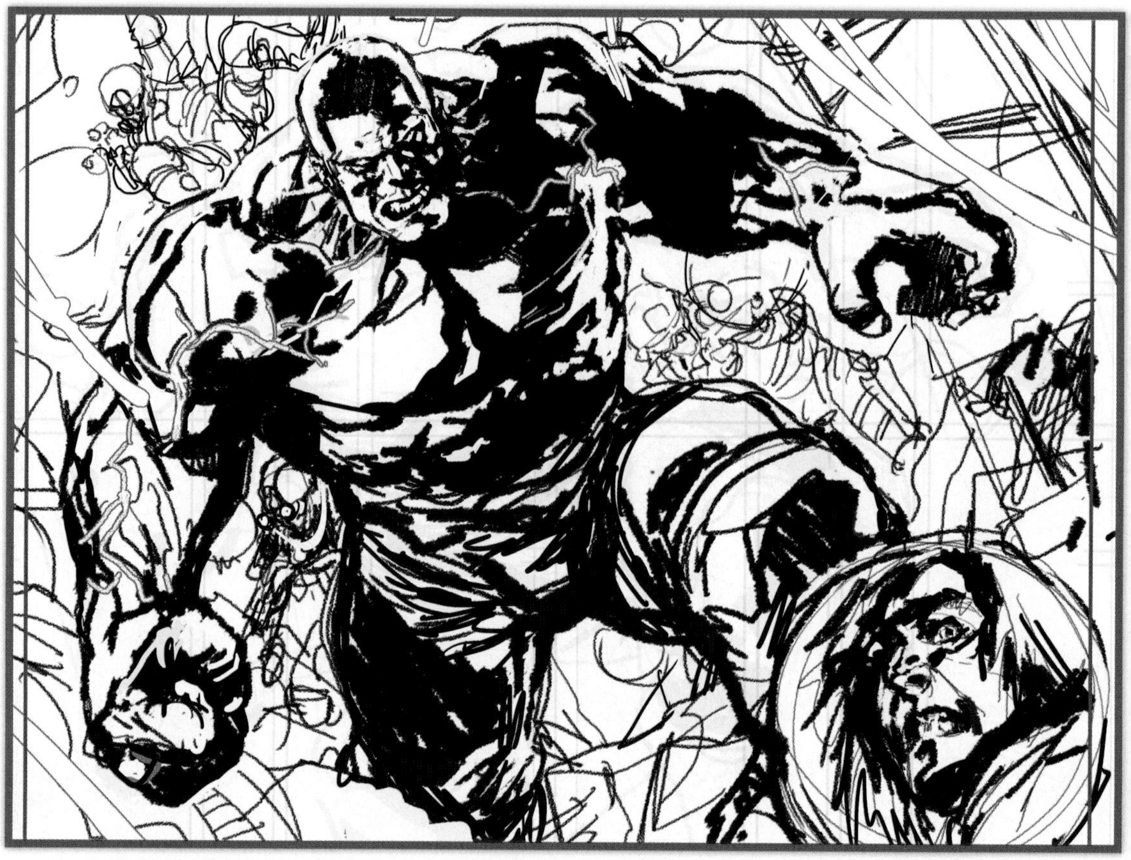

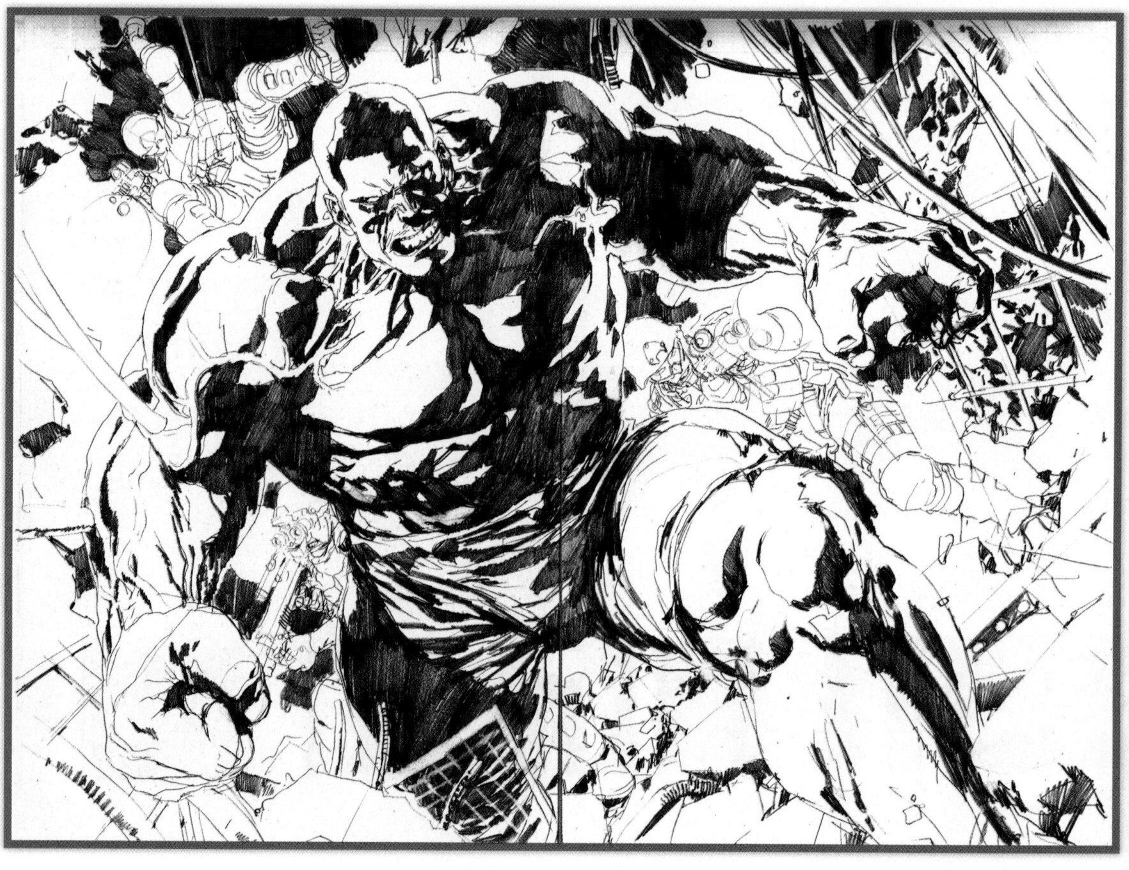

ISSUE #1, PAGES 12-13 ART PROCESS

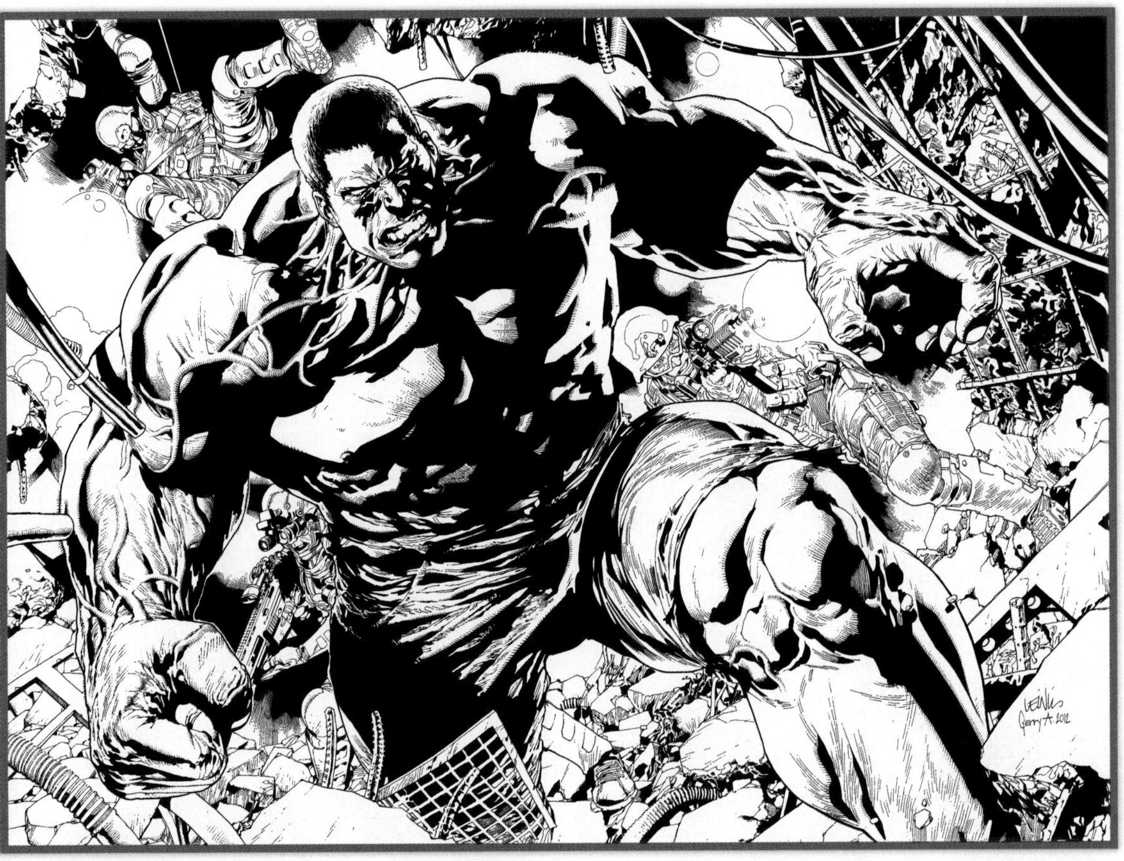

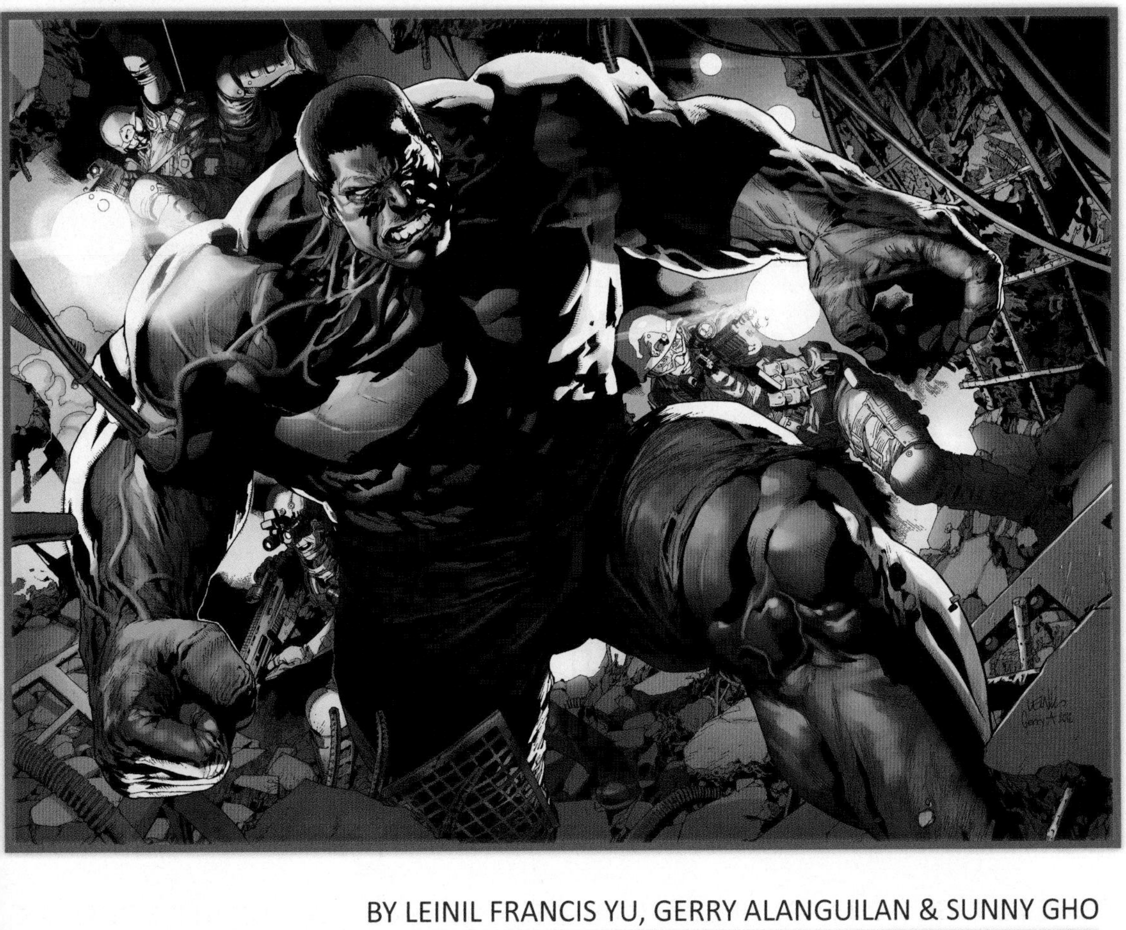

BY LEINIL FRANCIS YU, GERRY ALANGUILAN & SUNNY GHO

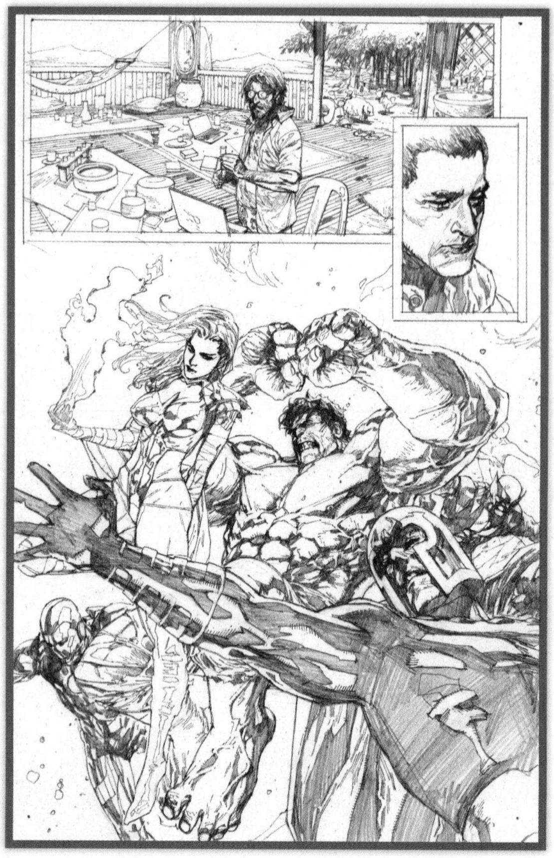

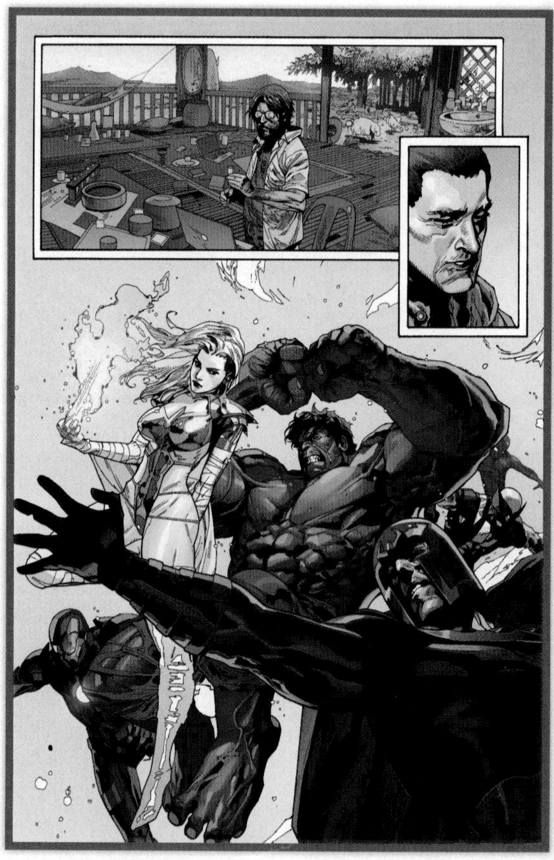

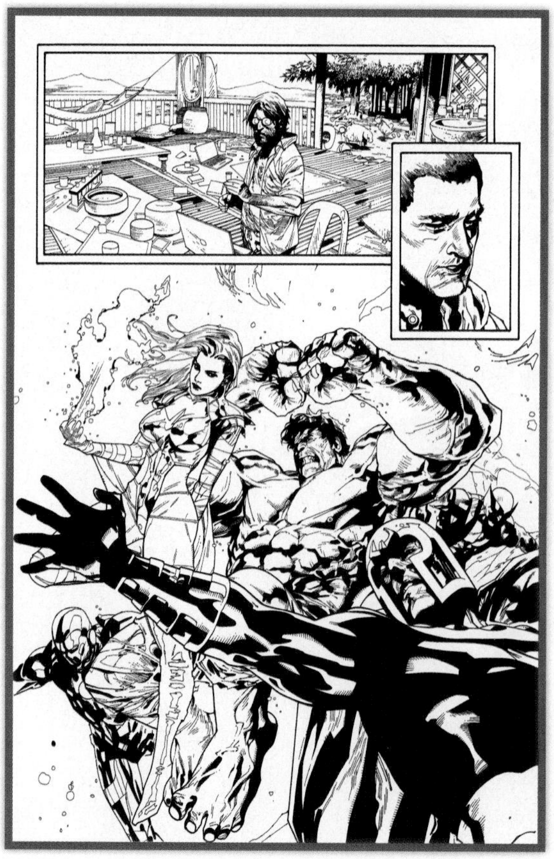

ISSUE #1, PAGE 5 ART PROCESS BY LEINIL FRANCIS YU, GERRY ALANGUILAN & SUNNY GHO

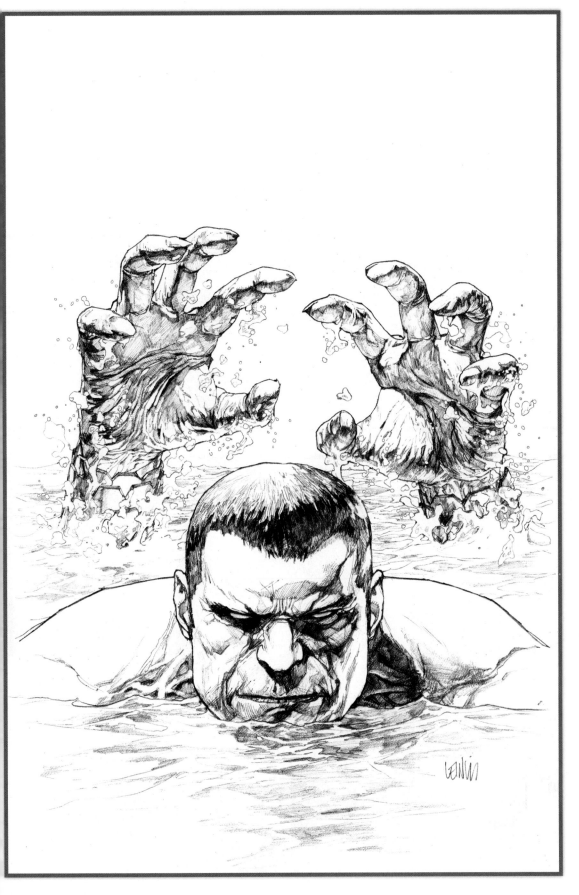

ISSUE #4 COVER PENCILS BY LEINIL FRANCIS YU

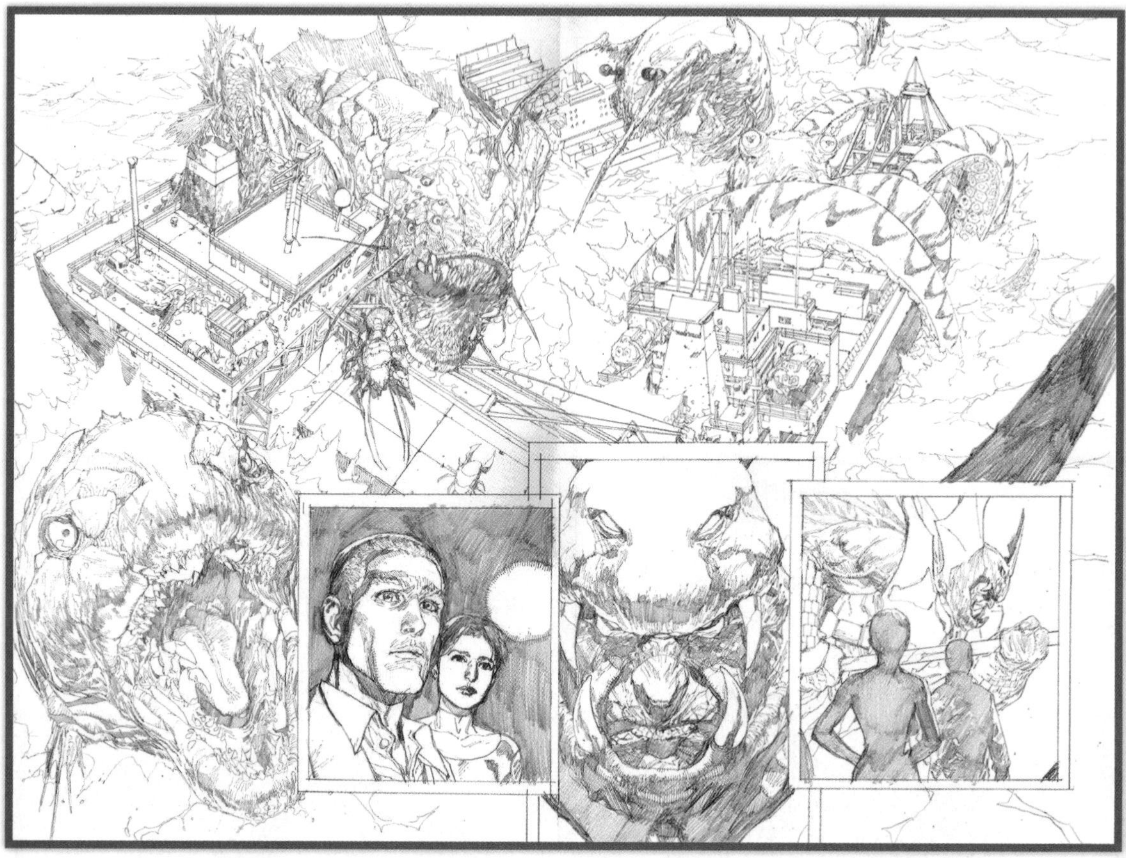

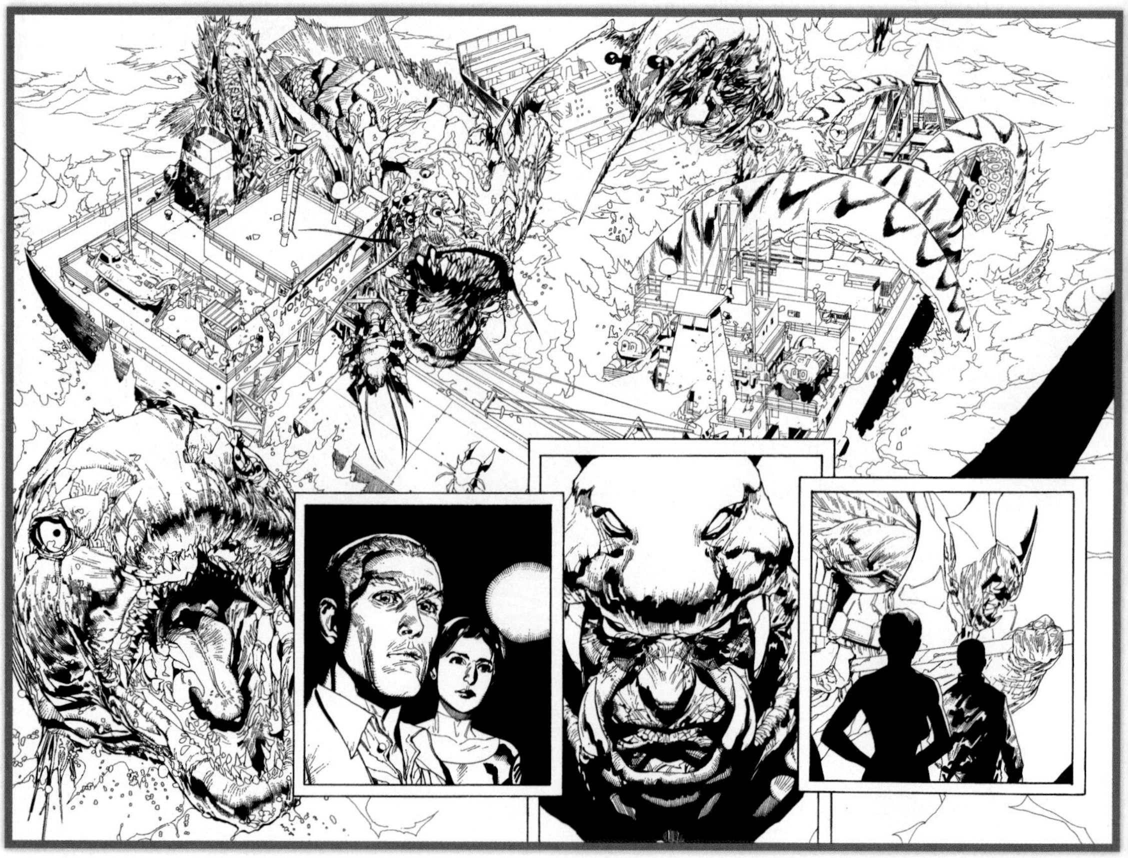

ISSUE #4, PAGES 8-9 ART PROCESS

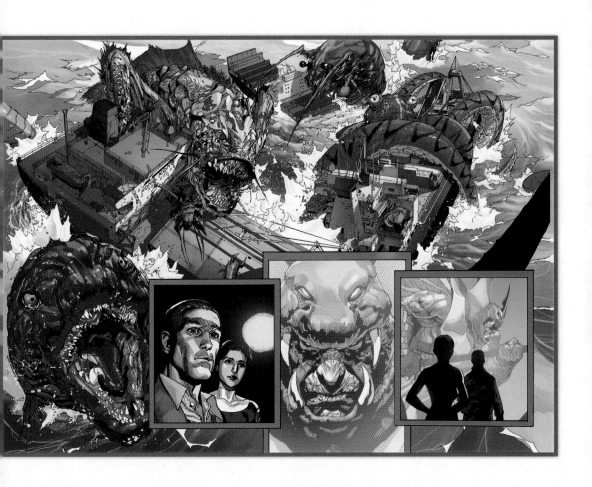

BY LEINIL FRANCIS YU, GERRY ALANGUILAN & SUNNY GHO

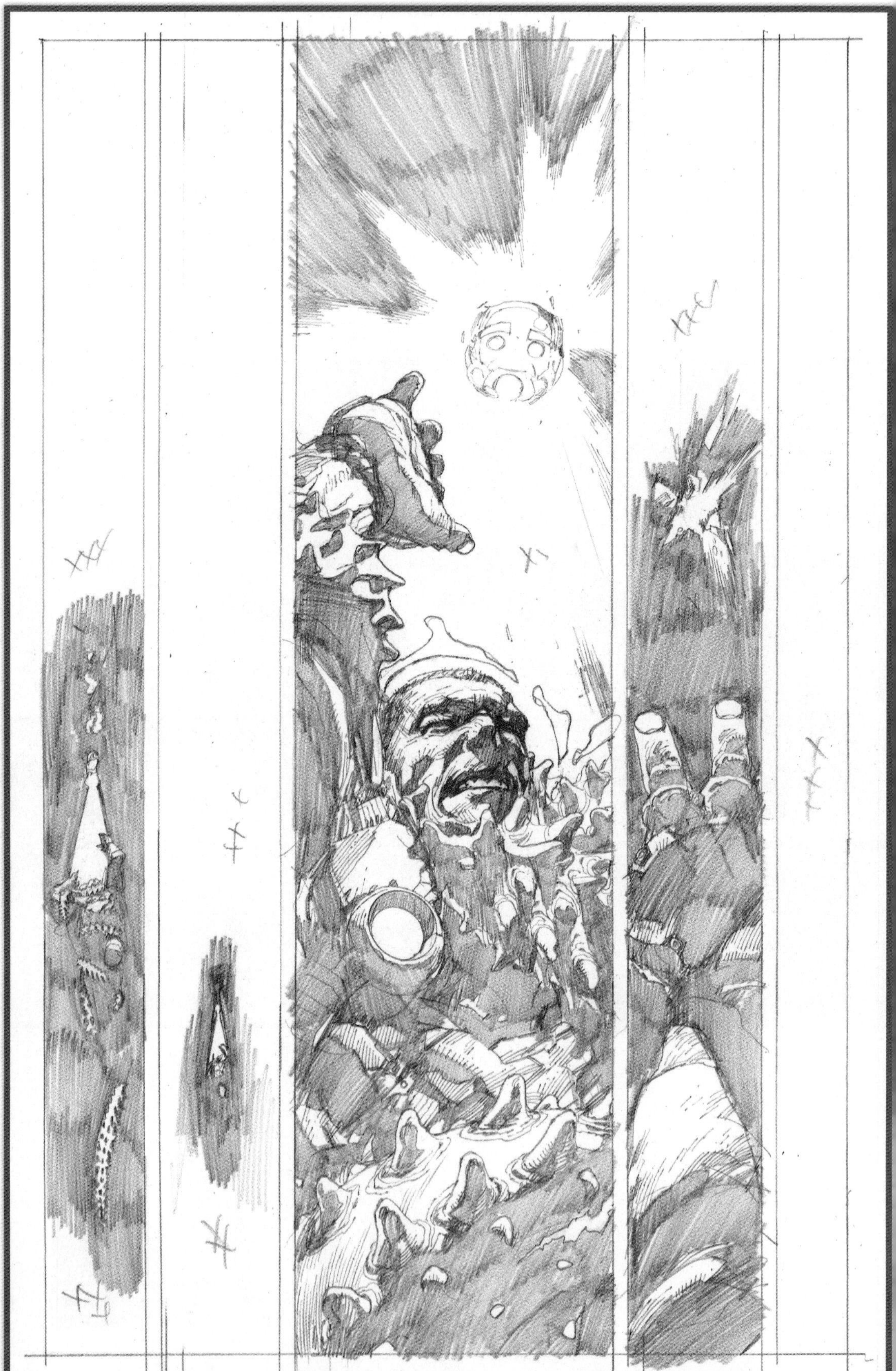

ISSUE #4, PAGE 19 ART PROCESS

BY LEINIL FRANCIS YU, GERRY ALANGUILAN & SUNNY GHO

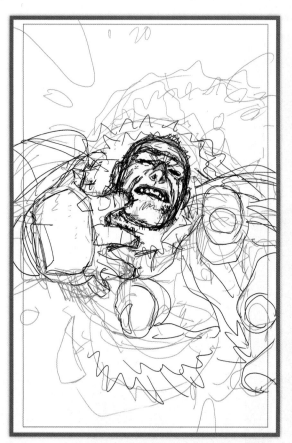

ISSUE #4, PAGE 20 ART PROCESS BY LEINIL FRANCIS YU, GERRY ALANGUILAN & SUNNY GHO

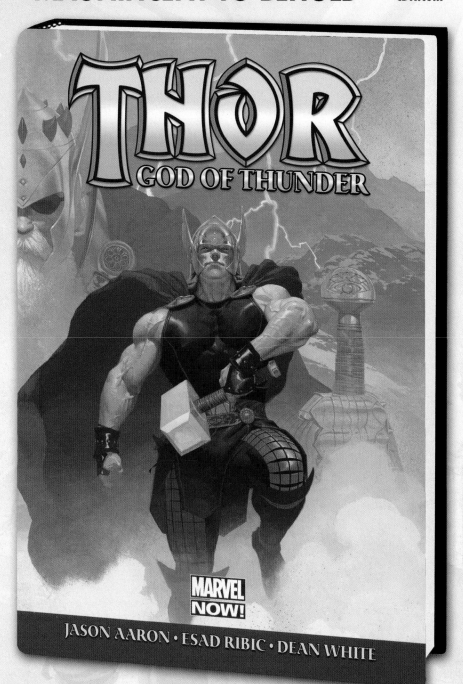

THE FREE *MARVEL AUGMENTED REALITY APP*
ENHANCES AND CHANGES THE WAY YOU EXPERIENCE COMICS!

To access the Marvel Augmented Reality App...

INDESTRUCTIBLE HULK **AR** INDEX